VC
HEROES

VC
HEROES

THE TRUE STORIES BEHIND EVERY VC
WINNER SINCE WORLD WAR TWO

NIGEL CAWTHORNE

JOHN BLAKE

Published by John Blake Publishing Ltd,
3 Bramber Court, 2 Bramber Road,
London W14 9PB, England

www.johnblakepublishing.co.uk

www.facebook.com/Johnblakepub   facebook

twitter.com/johnblakepub   twitter

First published in paperback as *Heroes* in 2007.
This edition published in paperback in 2012.

ISBN: 978 1 85782 810 8

British Library Cataloguing-in-Publication Data:

A catalogue record for this book is available from the British Library.

Design by www.envydesign.co.uk

Printed and bound in Great Britain by CPI Group (UK) Ltd

1 3 5 7 9 10 8 6 4 2

Papers used by John Blake Publishing are natural, recyclable products made
from wood grown in sustainable forests. The manufacturing processes
conform to the environmental regulations of the country of origin.

Every attempt has been made to contact the relevant copyright-holders,
but some were unobtainable. We would be grateful if the
appropriate people could contact us.

CONTENTS

INTRODUCTION

FOR VALOUR

The idea of giving a badge to be worn in recognition of bravery on the battlefield goes back to the ancient Greeks. The Roman legions then adopted it and established a standardised system of medals that they could wear on their uniforms. These were made of bronze or other metals and the images on them sometimes appeared on Roman gravestones.

The custom was continued by the Byzantine emperors and then picked up by Renaissance Italy and sixteenth-century Germany and seventeenth-century France. The first medals struck in England date back to the Civil War, when Charles I conferred gold medals on John Smith and Robert Welch for saving the King's Colours at the Battle of Edgehill in 1642. The following year, at Oxford, the king decreed that medals 'be delivered to wear on the breast of every man who shall be certified under the hands of their commanders-in-chief to have done faithful service in the forlorn hope'. Not to be outdone, the Parliamentarians picked up on the idea. The Commonwealth and, then, Charles II issued medals for gallantry in the Dutch Wars, but always on an ad hoc basis.

A standardised system of awards was introduced to the British Army during the Napoleonic Wars. Although some were given for bravery under fire, these were usually awarded for outstanding leadership or 'distinguished service' and restricted to officers. Meanwhile, the East India company introduced a fixed system of campaign medals for its Indian soldiers and, in 1837, instituted its own Order of Merit. This had three grades and, theoretically, a soldier had to have had a lower grade to be promoted to a higher one.

The British government was forced into introducing its own standardised system of awards for servicemen in the Crimean War. This was the first war to be reported in detail in the British press. War correspondents such as William Howard Russell of *The Times* brought home to the British public the terrible privations suffered by British soldiers and sailors, who were often poorly equipped and badly led – but could still be roused to extraordinary feats of bravery. Tales of the Charge of the Light Brigade, the Thin Red Line at Balaklava and life in the trenches in the Russian Winter during the siege of Sebastopol led to growing calls for the recognition of the bravery of British servicemen. In 1854, the Distinguished Conduct Medal was established by Royal Warrant to be conferred on 'other ranks' in the British Army, but not officers. The following year, the

Conspicuous Gallantry Medal was instituted by Order in Council for the non-officer ranks of the Royal Navy and Royal Marines. Officers' gallantry could always be recognised by admission to the Order of Bath or a mention in dispatches.

But even this did not slake the public's thirst for awards. The democratic sentiment of the time demanded an award that could be given in recognition of conspicuous bravery regardless of rank. In December 1854, Captain G T Scobell, MP for Bath, called in the House of Commons for the creation of 'an "Order of Merit" to be bestowed on persons serving in the Army or Navy for distinguished and prominent personal gallantry'. The Duke of Newcastle, then secretary for war, took the idea to Prince Albert, the Prince Consort. They looked abroad for inspiration. Britain and France were allies during the Crimean War and they decided that the new British award for gallantry should be modelled on the Legion of Honour, which had been created by Napoleon in 1802 and was conferred without regard to rank or religion. Queen Victoria herself favoured a single decoration without classes, open to all. But unlike the Legion of Honour, which could also be awarded for civic merit, the British award was open only to the military.

Names suggested for the new award included the Order of Valour and the Military Order of Victoria. Prince Albert came up with Victoria Cross. Then there was the motto to consider. 'The Reward for Valour' – the motto of the Indian Order of Merit – was one suggestion. Others included 'Reward for Bravery', 'For Bravery', 'To the Brave' and 'Mors aut Victoria' – 'Death or Victory'. Queen Victoria proposed 'For Valour'. It was to be awarded, the Royal Warrant said, 'only to those Officers or Men who have served Us in the presence of the Enemy and shall then have performed some signal act of valour or devotion to their Country'.

The Queen was also responsible for the simplicity of its design. She favoured the use of bronze over other, more opulent, options. They were made from the cascabels – the large knob at the back of a cannon used for securing ropes – of two Russian guns captured at Sebastopol. The two guns still stand outside the Rotunda of the Royal Arsenal at Woolwich, while the remainder of the metal is held in the Small Arms building of the Royal Logistic Corps' Defence Store at Donnington, Worcestershire. There is enough left to make 85 more medals.

Designed by the London jewellers Hancocks, the medal is in the form of the Army Gold Cross awarded in the final years of the Napoleonic Wars and since discontinued. The gunmetal was artificially darkened to give a greater contrast to the raised design when polished. On the front, there is the motto, the crown and a lion. On the back, they engraved the name, rank, service number and regiment or ship, along with date of the action it had been awarded for. *The Times* was not impressed. It said in the issue of 27 June 1857,

Than the Cross of Valour nothing could be more plain and homely, not to say coarse looking. It is a very small Maltese cross, formed from the gun-metal of ordnance captured at Sebastopol. In the centre is a small crown and lion, with which the latter's natural proportions of mane and tail the cutting of the cross much interferes. Below these is a small scroll (which shortens three arms of the cross and is utterly out of keeping with the upper portions) bearing the words 'For Valour'... the whole cross is, after all, poor looking and mean in the extreme... The merit of the design, we believe, is due to the same illustrious individual who once invented the hat.

However, the day before, when the first 62 medals were awarded for bravery in the Crimea, the Baltic and the Sea of Azov at the ceremony in Hyde Park, the public mobbed the recipients for a glimpse of the medal. Its award had been backdated to the beginning of the war. Nevertheless, *The Times* dismissed it as merely 'tuppence worth of bronze'. But that was the point. It was not supposed to be one of those precious, bejewelled baubles conferred by one aristocrat on another. In fact, the originals cost the government £1 to cast, with an additional three shillings (15p) for the engraving on the back.

The award brought with it a pension of £10 a year, with an additional £5 if a second Victoria Cross, or Bar, was awarded. The pension has now been increased to £1,495 a year. Additionally, all officers – however exalted their rank – were to salute the holder, if in uniform, no matter how lowly the recipient.

Soon after the first Victoria Crosses were awarded, the Queen became concerned about what the recipient should be called. Correct modes of address were all-important. She expressed her concern in a memo to the secretary for war, written in the regal third person.

'The Queen thinks that persons decorated with the Victoria Cross might very properly be allowed to bear some distinctive mark after their name,' she wrote. But the Victoria Cross was merely 'a naval and military decoration', not the membership of some distinguished order, as she was used to handing out. Consequently,

VC would not do. KG means a Knight of the Garter; CB a Companion of Bath; MP is a Member of Parliament; MD a Doctor of Medicine, etc., etc. – in all cases denoting a person. No one could be called a Victoria Cross. VC, moreover, means Vice-Chancellor at present. DVC, Decorated with the Victoria Cross, or BVC, Bearer of the Victoria Cross, might do. The Queen thinks the last is best.

However, VC caught on among both the military and civilians and remains the designation to this day.

Just a year after the VC was first awarded, it was extended to those members of the armed forces who showed

conspicuous courage and bravery… under circumstances of extreme danger, such as the occurrence of fire on board ship, or of the foundering of the vessel at sea, or under any other circumstance in which through the courage and devotion displayed, life or public property may be saved.

Then, in the face of the 'Indian Mutiny', its award was broadened to include civilians who fought alongside troops in the field or 'performed deeds of gallantry' against 'insurgent mutineers'. But, by 1881, it could again be awarded only for conspicuous courage in the face of the enemy. In 1902, Queen Victoria's son, King Edward, decreed that it could be awarded posthumously – as it was in many of the cases in this book. It remained open to anyone in any of the branches of the armed forces, including women, though no woman has yet received one.

The first VC was awarded to Lieutenant Charles Lucas of the Royal Navy for an action in the Baltic in 1854 when he ran forward to grab a live shell and throw it overboard, saving the crew of his ship HMS *Hecla*.

In all, 111 VCs were awarded during the Crimean War of 1854–6, which included naval engagements between Britain and Russia in the Baltic. A hundred and eighty-two were awarded during the Indian Mutiny of 1857–8, with another two awarded during the Bhutan Campaign to put down truculent Himalayan tribes in 1864–5. Sixteen were awarded during the various Afghan wars that rumbled on from 1838 to 1880, with seven more awarded during the Tirah Campaign of 1897–8 to secure the Khyber Pass. Then 23 were awarded during the Zulu War – eleven alone at Rorke's Drift, the largest for any single military action. The Transvaal War of 1880–1 produced six, the Matabeleland Rebellion of 1896 two and the Boer War of 1899–1900 78.

The Maori Wars of 1860–1 and 1863–6 produced fifteen. Three resulted from the Shimonoseki Expedition to Japan in 1864. Four were awarded during the Ashanti War of 1873–4. Three were given during the occupation of Egypt in 1882;

another three in First Sudan Campaign of 1881–5. One resulted from the Crete Rebellion of 1898. Six came from the Second Sudan Campaign of 1896–1900. Two resulted from the Boxer Uprising in 1900, three more from the Third Somaliland Expedition of 1903–4.

World War One produced 626. Ten more were awarded during various 'mopping-up' operations in India between World War One and World War Two. And 182 resulted from World War Two. In all, 1,341 had been awarded by the end of 1945. Since then there have been only fourteen recipients, due to the increasingly strict criteria applied. This book tells the stories of those fourteen gallant men.

PART I
KOREA

The Korean War was a direct consequence of the end of World War Two in the Far East. Throughout most of the war a non-aggression pact between the Soviet Union and Japan held. But on 8 August 1945 – two days after the first atomic bomb had been dropped on Hiroshima – the Soviet Union revoked the pact and declared war on Japan, invading Manchuria, seizing the northern part of Korea and taking more than 2 million Japanese prisoners before the Japanese capitulation on 15 August.

In an effort to disarm the Japanese Army and repatriate the estimated 700,000 Japanese who had gone to live in Korea since Japan occupied that country in 1905, the United States and the Soviet Union decided to divide the peninsula at the 38th parallel, formalising their zones of occupation. The Soviets quickly politicised the division by installing a hardline communist government in the North under Kim Il-sung, leader of the Korean contingent of the Soviet Red Army. US President Harry S Truman persuaded the newly founded United Nations to assume responsibility for Korea, while US troops guaranteed the military security of the South.

The UN then decided to set up an independent republic in South Korea, which led to a partisan uprising by communist guerrillas. When this failed, Kim Il-sung persuaded his sponsor, the Soviet leader Joseph Stalin, to back an invasion of the South. On 25 June 1950, the North Korean People's Army swept across the 38th parallel, taking the South Korean capital of Seoul and forcing the South Koreans and the Americans back to a small perimeter around the port of Pusan.

Truman returned to the UN and asked for member states to provide military assistance to the fledgling Republic of Korea. This could have been vetoed by the Soviet Union as a permanent member of the Security Council. However, the Soviets were boycotting the UN at the time in an attempt to get China's seat on the Security Council – occupied by the Nationalists, who were by then confined to the island of Taiwan – handed over to the representatives of the People's Republic in Beijing. Other nations, including France, Turkey, Belgium, Greece, the Netherlands, Colombia, Ethiopia, Thailand and the Philippines, sent soldiers to defend South Korea, while the British and Australians contributed a Commonwealth brigade. The entire United Nations force was under the command of the US General Douglas MacArthur.

The UN forces began to push the North Koreans back, then outflanked them with a successful amphibious landing at

In'chon on 14 September 1950, reoccupying Seoul soon after. MacArthur's forces crossed the 38th parallel and pursued the North Koreans almost to the Yalu river, which forms the border between North Korea and China.

In October 1950, the People's Republic of China entered the war on North Korea's side with Soviet air support. The UN forces were quickly pushed back deep into South Korea. MacArthur was sacked for having failed to limit the war in Korea and provoking the Chinese attack. He was replaced by General Matthew B Ridgway.

The war swung back and forth across the 38th parallel with huge casualties on both sides. It soon became clear that the war could be won by neither belligerent. On 8 July 1951, liaison officers from both sides met at the ancient capital of Kaesong on the front line. While they talked, the fighting continued. In October 1951, the talks were moved to a more secure area in the village named Panmunjom, where an armistice was signed on 27 July 1953. However, no peace treaty has ever been signed. Technically, despite the long-lasting truce, the two sides are still at war and meetings continue at Panmunjom.

This long and bloody struggle from stalemate to stalemate produced four VCs.

CHAPTER ONE

FRIENDLY FIRE

MAJOR KENNETH MUIR
23 September 1950, 1st Battalion, Argyll and Sutherland Highlanders
(Princess Louise's) (Posthumous)

In August 1950, the Argyll and Sutherland Highlanders were mustered in Hong Kong. While their commanding officer, Lieutenant Colonel George Neilson, and an advanced party travelled to Korea by United States transport plane, the 1st Battalion of the Argylls boarded the cruiser HMS *Ceylon* in Victoria Harbour under their second-in-command Major Kenneth Muir. Although full of trepidation, the men had enjoyed one last weekend of freedom among the bars and pretty girls of Kowloon.

At around 6.30 a.m. on 23 August, with the men secured below, the *Ceylon* began to move away from Holt's Wharf, played out by the pipe band of the King's Own Scottish Borderers and the Leicesters, both in full dress uniform. The pipes of the Argylls and the band of the Royal Marines responded from the *Ceylon's* quarterdeck. As they sailed out into the South China Sea, accompanied by the Middlesex Regiment on board the fleet support carrier *Unicorn* and escorted by the Australian destroyer *Warramunga*, the US transport with their commanding officers on board circled the ships and dropped a flare.

Before they had left Hong Kong, the Argylls had been issued with the latest 3.5-inch anti-tank rocket launcher to replace the 2.36-inch model, the original bazooka, which had not proved effective against the Soviet T34 tanks. They had also been issued with twenty rounds of live ammunition so that they could familiarise themselves with the weapon during the voyage. In Korea, they were to be part of the UN force that had been pushed back to a small toehold around Pusan. The British contingent were to be known as the 'Woolworth Brigade', because they relied on the Americans for everything, from rations to artillery and air support.

As they approached the quay at Pusan, the British contingent were greeted by US Army band playing the popular song 'Silver Dollar', which slipped tempo into 'God Save the King' as the *Ceylon* and *Unicorn* tied up. Then a Korean Army band and a choir of Korean schoolchildren joined in. Korean government officials and the press corps were there to greet them.

'They marched ashore as if they were still on parade. And they all looked fighting fit,' noted the *Daily Mail*.

The soldiers were young, though anyone in the regiment younger than 19 had been left behind in Hong Kong. Then the

Argyll pipers, in their distinctive white tunics and regimental kilts, struck up. An American journalist asked Lieutenant Colonel Andrew Man of the Middlesex Regiment why they had no band.

'Well, the Scots need those contraptions to fight with,' he replied.

Trains were waiting to carry them up to Kyongsan. The Royal Navy helped load their equipment, then the Argylls had to wait all day among the refugees who had fled the North and the stench of open sewers and the wood smoke of a thousand cooking fires. Finally, by 2330, they had boarded the train and it pulled out to carry them the 60 miles to Taegu.

As they were moving up into active service, the colours of the battalion, along with the regimental silver, had been left behind in Hong Kong, together with the heavy vehicles. The Americans were to supply the British, though this presented logistical problems. Despite a quayside speech about the 'historic unity of the Anglo-Saxon people', transatlantic ammunition calibres did not match and the US quartermasters had to search long and hard to find a special issue of tea that would suit British tastes.

For the next two weeks, living under makeshift shelters, the battalion survived on bread, cheese, cold sausage at midday and 'some form of exotic American tinned meat' for dinner. Winter clothing was held in reserve. The men kept fit by running or climbing the hills. They continued to practise with the new bazooka, while officers began liaison visits to the American units in the line.

On 4 September the British were moved into the line along

the Naktong River, relieving the 3rd Battalion of the American 23rd Infantry, holding the left flank of the US 1st Cavalry Division. They were to hold 10 miles of the 35-mile front there, supported by a platoon of Sherman tanks, a battery of 155mm artillery, one of 105mm guns and an attachment of Tactical Air Control from the 5th Air Force. The Argylls were to hold the southern sector, the Middlesex the north.

The handover was to be done at night, to avoid alerting the enemy. During the day, reconnaissance parties had been sent ahead. Then, at dusk, the main body was brought up on board US trucks. They set off in single file down mountain tracks that soon petered out. After that, they navigated by compass, making as little noise as possible. This was not without its difficulties on hillsides coved with scrub and dwarf oaks. The advance was covered by Vickers medium machine guns and 3-inch mortars. But there were such gaps in the defensive cover that the enemy could come and go unseen.

By sunrise the Argylls were in position, though they had not been helped by their American guides, who had lost their way. The Middlesex were in more trouble. A subaltern returning to his platoon after a recce was shot by a sentry. On 8 September their vehicles arrived, having been bought my merchant ship from Hong Kong and by railway flatcar from Pusan.

With American and Republic of Korea troops fighting defensive actions to either side, the British set up listening posts on either side of the Naktong River and sent out reconnaissance patrols at night. They soon discovered that a large force of the North Korean People's Army was forming up on the hills to the south of the Argylls. One early patrol engaged one of its outposts and American artillery and British mortars pummelled the enemy's position.

The Argylls' left flank was difficult to supply. Air drops were not accurate enough and supplies had to be brought up by Korean porters. American helicopters medevacked the wounded out. Some 230 poorly armed and badly trained Korean policemen were brought up to fill the gap between the British and the US 2nd Division to the south. An ex-World War Two prisoner of war was chosen to liaise with them because he spoke some Japanese, a language widely understood by Koreans after Japan's long occupation.

On the night of 20 September, the British crossed the Naktong in force in an effort to begin the breakout from the Pusan perimeter. After they had established a forward position the other side of the river, the first objective was to take the high ground beyond. That afternoon, with the support of two US Sherman tanks, A Company managed to take Hill 148 without losing a man. But there was not enough time before nightfall to take to the two hills – Hill 282 and Hill 388 – that formed ends of a ridge about a mile long beyond.

During the night of the 22nd, the British brought up mortars and Vickers machine guns to guard the flanks, and American forward artillery observers joined the Argylls. Colonel Neilson set up his headquarters at the eastern end of a ridge held by A Company, which overlooked B and C Companies' start line for the next day's assault. The Argylls were told that they would be making a surprise attack, so there would be no artillery softening up or preliminary aerial bombardment that might warn the enemy of their intentions.

Although they had spent most of the night digging in, the 1st Battalion of the Argyll and Sutherland Highlanders were woken at 0400 and drawn up facing northwest and the spurs that led up to Hill 282. There was a slight delay while they waited for a platoon that had got lost in the darkness. Then they finally set off at 0520.

All was quiet as they crossed a dry rice paddy and started their ascent. About halfway up, there were several bursts of fire from above. But this was probably just a response to noise heard from below. After a brief halt, the advance began again. It was hard going, since the hill was steep and covered with scrub, loose rocks and fir trees. But at 0550, just as dawn was breaking, B Company reached an open stretch just below the final ridge. There they surprised a bunch of North Korean soldiers having breakfast in the open just 100 yards from the summit.

'The North Koreans were not used to being attacked at 5 a.m. and the leading Argylls were able to get within 50 yards before making their charge,' said one of the Argylls who was there.

Those who stood and fought were killed. Others made off, dragging their wounded behind them. The firing alerted another Korean position that the Argylls had passed in the darkness. They opened fire with everything they had, so B Company had to turn back to clear it. Fifteen NKPA soldiers were killed for the loss of five wounded and one dead – a platoon commander. Then followed a classic 'highland charge'. Screaming like banshees, the

Argylls used their rifles and bayonets to clear the North Korean positions. The aggression of the Scots regiment was too much for the NKPA and those who were left alive fled. At 0618 Major Alastair Gordon-Ingram, the commander of B Company, could report back that they had taken Hill 282, at the cost of another ten casualties.

At 0630, C Company, under Major J M Gillies arrived, minus a platoon, which had already joined B Company. They deployed along the ridge, digging slit trenches and collecting the wounded for evacuation. This would be difficult, because the hillside was too steep for stretchers. To get the wounded down, each would have to be carried by four men holding a ground sheet. In the meantime, a request was sent for extra morphine.

Colonel Neilson then ordered Major Gillies to take Hill 388 at the other end of the ridge. This lay 2,000 yards away across a low saddle. But, first, defensive positions had to be completed and an artillery plan drawn up. At 0815, battalion headquarters moved up to Hill 148 and A Company was stood down for a wash and breakfast. Then at 0830 ranging fire of North Korean mortars began to rain down, but the ridge-top defences were almost complete, minimising British casualties. Half an hour later, small parties of North Koreans began infiltrating around the left flank and the British forward position had to be reinforced.

For Major Kenneth Muir, the position of second-in-command was a frustrating one. In the ordinary course of events, all he could do was wait until his superior officer was sick, wounded, killed or in some other way incapacitated. But Major Muir was a man of action and, when a carrier party sent forward to evacuate the wounded got lost, he volunteered to lead a second team. By 0900, he was at the top of Hill 282 and in the thick of it.

Having established the range, the enemy were now bombarding the ridge with mortar and shell fire. The weather was not good, but the Americans were trying to get a Mosquito spotter plane airborne to find out where the enemy guns were. In the meantime, they were shelling Hill 388 in the hope of dislodging a possible artillery observation post there.

As the North Korean bombardment continued, there were soon nearly thirty British casualties, more than Muir and his party could handle. It was as much as they could do to move them to the collection point. Then at 0930 the British were informed that the American artillery support would have to be withdrawn, because it was needed elsewhere. They protested, but were assured that the American batteries would continue their support until some relief was found. In fact, the guns were already on the move and the Argylls were left with no weapons with the range to reach the North Korean positions on Hill 388 that overlooked them.

On the ridge, C Company reported what they thought was a small force approaching through the scrub. Things were no better to the rear, where A Company encountered the NKPA coming in from the southwest and west, and found themselves in a battle to hold onto Hill 148.

C Company then found that they were under full attack by a much larger force than they had imagined.

'The scrub is full of them,' they radioed.

Two sections of B Company moved forward to reinforce them while the battalion pummelled the scrub with 3-inch mortars. Two Bren guns held back the frontal attack, but the North Koreans began another flanking action. For the next hour this infiltration increased, as did the shelling and mortaring, causing further casualties to the two companies.

Major Muir, a natural leader, took charge and consolidated his forces in the perimeter on Baker Ridge, being held by C Company. According to one report,

Major Muir, although only visiting the position, automatically took over command and with complete disregard for his own personal safety started to move around the forward elements, cheering on and encouraging the men to greater efforts despite the fact that ammunition was running low. He was continually under fire, and despite entreaties from officers and men alike, refused to take cover.

In fact, after assessing the situation, he had radioed Colonel Neilson and proposed that he take command of the hilltop defences. He was confident that he could hold Hill 282, he said, provided they were well supplied with ammunition. However, they were sitting ducks for enemy artillery and mortar fire, and could promise no offensive action unless he was given fire support.

Colonel Neilson immediately agreed that Major Muir should take command on Hill 282. Ammunition was on its way, carried by C Company's returning stretcher bearers, and Neilson said he had already requested an airstrike on Hill 388, sending full map references. Then the news came through that three American Mustangs would strike at noon.

As the Argylls waited on the hilltop, under fire, for the American airstrike, they laid out large white panels, indicating the presence of friendly troops. At midday, a Mosquito spotter plane appeared above the ridge. The ground troops had no means of communicating with it, but its presence comforted them, since it indicated that help was on its way. In fact, the American forward air controller sent to coordinate the attacks was on the ground at an observation point some way behind.

At 1215, the three Mustangs came roaring in. They circled, looking over the ground. Then they formed a single file and began their attack. They came in low, guns blazing, dropping tanks of napalm. But these hit not Hill 388 but Hill 282. Baker Ridge exploded in a plume of flame a billowing black smoke.

'I've never seen anything as black, even as a fireman,' said Pat Quinn, an Argyll on the hill who went on to become a fire-fighter in Greater Manchester.

As the hilltop was engulfed in a sea of orange flame, survivors plunged 15 metres (50 feet) down the slope to escape the burning napalm. Then the Mustangs turned for a second run. Major Muir jumped to his feet and waved the white panel. But it did no good. This time the Mustangs fired rockets into the ridge. Then they pulled away and attacked A Company on Hill 148. It was all over in about five minutes.

Some of the wounded had been killed. Fresh wounded made

their way to the collection point, if they could. Those badly burned had to be carried.

With the main defensive position destroyed, the Argylls withdrew to a position some 15 metres (50 feet) below the crest.

'There is no doubt that a complete retreat from the hill would have been fully justified at the time,' it was reported in dispatches.

But Major Muir was not going to give up the hill. He realised that the enemy had not taken immediate advantage of the incident and the crest was still unoccupied, although under fire.

'I'll take them up again, and this time we'll stay,' said Muir.

According to Major David Wilson, the commanding officer of A Company and the last man to talk to Major Muir on the battalion net, 'He said he was going to get the summit back to give the wounded a chance… and in the style of the Northwest Frontier somehow got back to the top. I have never seen anything like it. From perhaps 2,000 yards away, I watched through by glasses, impotent to do anything.'

Major Muir mustered Major Gordon-Ingram, Captain Penman, Company Sergeant Major Collett and some six soldiers, and moved forward. As the flames subsided, they saw Private Watts, who had somehow survived, firing on the approaching enemy from a rocky outcrop. To their surprise, the ridge was still in Argyll hands.

With Major Gillies giving covering fire, Major Muir mustered what men he could and led them forward, cheering, to join Private Watts. According to dispatches, Major Muir personally led the counter-attack on the crest. To appreciate fully the implication of this, it is necessary to realise how demoralising the effect of the air-strike had been and it was entirely due to his courage, determination and splendid example of this officer that such a counter-attack was possible. All ranks responded magnificently and the crest was retaken.

The NKPA were driven back, but they remained in a position to harry the Argylls with small-arms fire. Nevertheless, Muir was in a position to radio Colonel Neilson and tell him that he still held the hilltop.

Neilson gave Muir permission to hold his position or withdraw, as he saw fit. But Muir was in no mood for retreat, particularly now he had been reinforced by the returning stretcher bearers, who went scavenging among the dead for weapons.

Soon the North Koreans were advancing through the scrub again. They were greeted with a barrage of small-arms fire. Major Muir's VC citation says:

From this moment on, Major Muir's actions were beyond all possible praise. He was determined that the wounded would have adequate time to be taken out and he was just as determined that the enemy would not take the crest. Grossly outnumbered and under heavy automatic fire, Major Muir moved about his small force, redistributing fast diminishing ammunition.

Major Muir's personal leadership and courage inspired the defenders who held the ridge for half an hour in the face of overwhelming odds. When ammunition for his own weapon ran out, Major Muir teamed up with Major Gordon-Ingram to man a 2-inch mortar 'with very great effect against the enemy'. While firing the mortar, Major Muir was still shouting encouragement and advice to his men, and for a further five minutes the enemy were held at bay.

'Finally, Major Muir was hit with two bursts of automatic fire which mortally wounded him,' the official dispatches recorded, 'but he retained consciousness and was still determined to fight on.'

'Neither the gooks nor the US Air Force will drive the Argylls off this hill,' were his last reported words.

Supported by 3-inch mortars from below, the Argylls drove the NKPA back. At the end of the action, Major Gordon-Ingram found he had only ten men left fit to fight – and three of them were wounded. With just three Brens and enough ammunition for a magazine each, they withdrew to Charlie Ridge, where Major Gillies had roughly the same strength, dragging their wounded comrades behind them.

With their ammunition exhausted and scarcely a man who was not wounded, Major Gordon-Ingram then radioed Colonel Neilson, asking for permission to withdraw and requesting stretcher bearers. Neilson said that forty or fifty men were already on their way. These included clerks, pipers, drivers, the adjutant and intelligence officer from battalion headquarters, along with volunteers from the Middlesex regiment, whose first-aid post also handled the Argylls' wounded.

'The battle-exhausted survivors came down the hill carrying or dragging the wounded,' said Pat Quinn. 'I was so badly wounded that I could not walk and had to be dragged down the hill, but at least I was still alive… The worst part of it all was the napalm. Even as a fireman I have never seen anything like the destruction that stuff does to human skin. I never want to hear of that stuff being used again.'

On Hill 282, Major Gordon-Ingram's men searched for anyone left alive. Finding none, they pulled back under the covering fire of Major Gillies's men. By 1500, the survivors were back down at the foot of the hill. When the company rolls had been checked, the losses totalled around ninety. However, in the heat of battle, men sometimes get lost and it is customary to wait 72 hours until they are posted missing. In fact, two men found their way back off Hill 282 the following day. The Argylls' losses were 17 killed, including Major Muir, and 79 wounded, including one injured earlier crossing the Naktong. Around 60 of the casualties were due to the Americans' 'friendly fire'. The battalion was quickly reorganised into two rifle companies and settled for the night on Hill 148, waiting for whatever the next day would bring. There would be no more fighting for Hill 282, though. Later that day the North Koreans withdrew.

On the 25th, the Argylls joined the advance on Sonju. By the end of the month, the NKPA line had split open. The Argylls found themselves mopping up stragglers and taking arms caches disclosed to them by villagers. By the 28th, they were reinforced by other Highland regiments.

Meanwhile, the head of the British 27 Brigade, Brigadier Basil

Coad, had written to General MacArthur, requesting an explanation of the disastrous airstrike on the Argylls by the 5th US Air Force. Air Vice-Marshal Cecil Bouchier, senior British liaison officer with the commander-in-chief of the UN forces, asked Major-General Earle Partridge, commanding officer of the 5th Air Force, for an account. He was told that the forward air controllers were not close enough to Hill 282 because they could not get across a small river and the spotter plane used a different scale of map. The officer in charge of the ground-control team had told the Mustangs that the enemy often copied allied recognition panels, so they should ignore those on Hill 282. He had been replaced.

During the following weeks, efforts were made by the US authorities and private individuals to make amends and, according to the Argyll and Sutherland Highlanders' own official history, 'the reputation of the battalion was if anything enhanced by the tragedy'.

Both the British and Americans tried to hold back the names of those injured by 'friendly fire' during the airstrike. However, the press had already got pictures. *Time* magazine carried the story and it was too late to stage a cover-up.

Announcing Major Muir's posthumous award of the Victoria Cross, the *London Gazette* of 5 January 1951 said,

The effect of his splendid leadership on the men was nothing short of amazing and it was entirely due to his magnificent courage and example and the spirit of which he imbued in those about him that all wounded were evacuated from the hill, and, as was subsequently discovered, very heavy casualties inflicted on the enemy in the defence of the crest.

Born in Chester on 6 March 1912, Major Kenneth Muir had come from an Army family. A short, stocky man, he had never thought to do anything else but follow his father into the Argyll and Sutherland Highlanders. He was commissioned in 1932 and saw active service on the Northwest Frontier of India from 1935 to 1938. There, it is said, he learned the golden rules of regimental soldiering: always occupy the hilltops; never let the enemy dominate you from higher ground; never leave your wounded behind.

During World War Two, he rose from captain to acting Lieutenant Colonel and saw active service, some of it attached to the military police, in the Sudan, north Africa, Italy, France and Germany. By the end of the war he had earned eight campaign medals and a mention in dispatches. After a spell in the provost marshal's branch of the War Office, he was sent to Hong Kong as second-in-command of the Argylls. He was buried in the United Nations Memorial Cemetery in Pusan, South Korea. The Americans were the first to honour Major Muir with the posthumous award of the Distinguished Service Cross.

On 14 February 1951, Major Muir's father, Lieutenant Colonel Garnet Wolsey Muir, who had been commander of the Argylls from 1923 to 1927, went to Buckingham Palace to receive the Victoria Cross from King George VI on his son's behalf. Afterwards he said, 'I am proud beyond all words. My son, my only son, was a soldier all the way.'

However, crippled with grief and depression, Muir's father took his own life three years later.

In March 2004, Major Muir's name appeared on a war memorial unveiled at Malvern College, commemorating former pupils who died fighting for their country. He had attended the school from 1926 to 1929. His name was joined by that of RAF Wing Commander Nigel Elsdon, who died in a Tornado while leading the 27 Squadron bombing of an Iraqi airfield during the first Gulf War. The memorial has been left open-ended, so names can be added in the event of further losses.

CHAPTER TWO

GLOSTERS' HILL

LIEUTENANT COLONEL JAMES POWER CARNE DSO
22–25 April 1951, 1st Battalion, Gloucestershire Regiment

LIEUTENANT PHILIP CURTIS
22–23 April 1951, Duke of Cornwall's Light Infantry, attached to 1st
Battalion, Gloucestershire Regiment (Posthumous)

Lieutenant Colonel James 'Fred' Carne was the first commanding officer of the 5th Battalion (TA) when it was re-formed after World War Two. After serving as the 43rd Reconnaissance Regiment in Normandy and northwest Europe, the 5th was recommissioned on 1 March 1947 and had its colours restored at a service in Gloucester Cathedral on 18 January 1948.

In his address, the Chaplain-General of the Forces said, 'These colours represent the traditions of a regiment which go back to 1694. For 250 years the swirl of the Severn, the calm of the Cotswolds, and the constancy of this Cathedral have been your blood and story. The old 28th, impetuous as the Severn, swirled into the fight with their short swords when they had not a shot left, and were called the "slashers"; calm as the Cotswolds, attacked on all sides, they fought back to back in Egypt; constant as this Cathedral, the old 61st was known from the number of their scarlet dead as "the Flowers of Toulouse".'

On a Wednesday afternoon in mid-July 1950, Colonel Carne was watching a cricket match when the adjutant arrived with a signal marked 'Secret'. Carne read it calmly. It said that the 29th Brigade were to mobilise at once for action in Korea. Commanding officers were to report their requirements for officers and men. But, as the government had not yet made the announcement that Britain was, once again, going to war, the orders were to be known by as few people as possible.

'Well, it's not entirely unexpected,' Carne told the adjutant. 'I'll come back to the office.'

It was no surprise because Britain had already committed herself in the United Nations Security Council to supporting South Korea against the invasion from the North. American troops were already arriving in South Korea. The British were bound to follow, and who else would they send but a battalion that had been trained as part of the 'imperial strategic reserve'?

The Glosters were not up to strength. There was conscription at the time, but not all national servicemen would be able to go. Reservists had to be called up and passed fit, then the regular soldiers, national servicemen and reservists – each constituting about a third of the battalion's strength – would have to undergo an intensive programme of training so that they could work together.

Following a brief embarkation leave, they were inspected by the Chief of the Imperial General Staff, Field Marshal Sir William Slim. Then the advanced party flew to Korea to fight alongside the Americans while the remainder embarked on troop ships at Southampton on 7 October 1950. The *Cheltenham Chronicle* and the *Gloucester Echo* reported,

> As their gleaming white transport, *Empire Windrush*, sheered away from the quayside and thrust her bows into the grey reaches of Southampton Water, men of the 1st Battalion, The Gloucestershire Regiment, waved and cheer au revoir to England. The band of the Gloucestershire Regiment played on the quayside as the men went aboard, and there was a roar from the men lining the rails as the band broke into the strains of 'Far Away Places'.

Southampton had seen nothing like it for over fifty years. During the two World Wars, departing troop ships had slipped out of dock silently at night for fear of submarines or giving away vital intelligence. With the regimental band playing, the Union Jack waving, crowds cheering and relatives weeping, the khaki-clad soldiers could have been Queen Victoria's men off to fight in the Boer War. Leading the departure ceremony was the Colonel of the Regiment, Lieutenant General Sir Edward Wetherall, Lady

Wetherall, Lieutenant General Sir Ouvry Roberts and Lieutenant General Sir Gerald Templer, general officer commanding the Southern and Eastern Commands respectively. Alongside them were the wives of Privates Chamberlain and Thomas, who had got married on embarkation leave.

The mood on board ship was buoyant. The war seemed to be nearly over. The North Korean People's Army had been smashed. The very day the Glosters set sail, US forces had crossed the 38th parallel into North Korea and the UN General Assembly announced that it was to occupy the whole of the north and destroy the NKPA, to prevent any further attempt to reunify the country by force. The Glosters felt that there may be a little mopping-up to be done or some anti-guerrilla work, along with marching in the victory parades. There was one thing that everyone agreed on: they would be home by Christmas. They did not foresee that, as the UN forces neared the Yalu River marking the border with China, the Chinese would join the war on the side of the North Koreans.

Despite the carefree mood of his men, Colonel Carne was determined that they would arrive in Korea fit and ready for immediate action, if need be. There was to be physical training and weapons training every day. But then the men had brief stops at Port Said, Aden, Colombo and Singapore to look forward to. However, as they sailed east, they began to hear rumours of Chinese troops massing on the Manchurian border. As they approached the mountainous Korean coastline, partly obscured by squalls of driving rain, the news came that the People's Republic of China had entered the war.

This had not happened suddenly. When the UN forces first crossed the 38th parallel, the Chinese warned that they would not 'stand idly by', though they still sought assurances from Stalin that he would extend Soviet air cover to include Manchuria. On 15 October, Chinese troops crossed the border thinly disguised as volunteers. Then, on 24 October, three Chinese armies crossed the Yalu, followed almost immediately by another seven armies, while three more mustered in Manchuria. In all, more than 850,000 Chinese troops were committed, and at least 50,000 of these were front-line troops. They were hardened by years of fighting the Japanese and the Chinese Nationalists in the civil war that had ended only the year before. Having lived through every sort of atrocity, they fought on a bag of rice a day and continued their attack no matter how great their losses.

In the officers' lounge on the *Empire Windrush*, the Battalion's Intelligence Officer, Lieutenant Henry Cabral, kept a war map, showing the rapid Chinese advances, and it quickly became clear to Colonel Carne and his men that they were going to have to do a lot more than occupation duties. They were up against a formidable foe. As General Hobart Gay announced, melodramatically, when the commander of the British forces Brigadier Aubrey Coad visited the headquarters of the 1st US Cavalry Division, 'The Chinese are coming in. The Third World War has started.'

That was not entirely true, but Colonel Carne and his men knew they were about to face warfare as gruelling and vicious as anything they had seen in World War Two.

Pusan was no Western-style seaport. It was a harbour with the shanty town attached. It had nothing in the way of drainage and reeked of rotting refuse and human excrement. Nevertheless, it put on a show for the Glosters. The town was bedecked with flags – Union Flags, Stars and Stripes, the dove of the UN and the red-and-blue yin–yang sphere and black bars of the Republic of Korea. There was a Korean girls' choir in spotless white blouses and blue skirts to greet them, along with children waving tiny Union Flags.

Colonel Carne and the captain of the *Empire Windrush* disembarked to be greeted officially by a major of the United States Army. Carne was presented with a bouquet of gladioli, which he had to clutch through the welcoming ceremony, feeling 'like a complete idiot'.

The Americans had laid on a black military band, which played 'Tiger Rag', 'St Louis Blues', 'Chicago Tribune March' and 'The Marine Corps Hymn', under the baton of a seven-foot-tall drum major. A natural jazzman, he finished 'The Marine Corps Hymn' with a flourish of drums, cymbals and trombones, and a gigantic grin. The band then extended the compliment to the British by playing 'Colonel Bogey' in an exaggerated ragtime, while the drum major led them off at a march approximately twice the speed of a British rifleman's quickstep. Throughout it all, Colonel Carne fiddled self-consciously with his gladioli.

It was drizzling and cold on the evening of 11 November, when the Glosters boarded a filthy train at the corrugated-iron-roofed sheds that passed for a train station. Inside they squeezed themselves onto hard wooden benches in a compartment crammed with kitbags and other equipment. The small train seemed barely up to the task of hauling the overladen troop train. It was impossible to sleep and, when the drizzle stopped, the carriages filled with choking yellow dust. The train jerked and creaked its way up the Korean peninsula, making unexplained stops on the way.

Tea was brewed in tin hung outside the coach, and food was prepared on a station platform or alongside the tracks whenever the train stopped long enough. The menu consisted of bully beef, dehydrated potatoes and biscuits hard enough to break your teeth. Then there was the fearful indecision over whether the stop would be long enough to answer call of nature.

As the journey dragged on mile after bone-jarring mile, the young soldiers gazed in awed fascination over the paddy fields and stark hills, while the veterans remarked that, like almost everywhere they had visited during World War Two, it was not worth the visit. And everywhere they saw the aftermath of war – burned-out tanks, overturned trucks, bombed-out buildings, craters, rubble and endless lines of miserable, shuffling refugees, who fought each other for the biscuits and chocolate the soldiers flung from the windows.

Finally, on 14 November, the train pulled up to the broken platform at Suwon, where it was greeted by the familiar faces of the advance party. It had taken three days to cover less than two hundred miles. The Glosters then moved off to their quarters in the grand buildings of an agricultural college. That night autumn turned to winter. A freezing wind blew down from Siberia. The thermometer registered 22 degrees of frost – though the Glosters would eventually see it go down to minus 13°F. They found that the plywood nailed across the windows could not keep the cold out, nor could the fires that filled the buildings with smoke take off the chill.

Outside, the paddy fields and rivers froze. Eggs froze in their shells. Water tipped from a jug would freeze before it hit the ground. A cup of tea put down for ten seconds would turn into brown ice. Even making tea was an ordeal. It took water an hour and a half to boil. A tin of meat had to be immersed for two hours before it became even lukewarm.

Boiling water poured into a vehicle's radiator turned to ice almost immediately. Even Russian antifreeze captured from the North Koreans, which was supposed to work even in the depths of Siberia, simply froze. The oil used to lubricate rifles and machine guns turned solid after application. Touching anything metal took the skin off, making shaving a torment, though men did shave off their moustaches, otherwise they found inch-long icicles dangling from the hair.

The first thing that Carne did was organise an exercise in square bashing called, inevitably, 'First Frost' for those who had forgotten how to march on board ship. Then on 14 November, with woefully inadequate winter clothing, the battalion were moved north to Kaesong for anti-guerrilla duties. They were to mop up a detachment of North Koreans who had been bypassed as the Americans had pushed headlong for the Yalu River.

They headed north by train and somehow got divided into three parts by Korean National Railways – one party consisting solely of company commanders. D Company were dropped off to guard the bridges crossing the Imjin River at Munsan'ni, relieving a Turkish battalion. A and C Companies headed north into the heart of guerrilla country and established a redoubt at Sibyon'ni, while B Company and headquarters stayed at Kaesong. A and C Companies then made sweeps through the outlying regions, but their intelligence was inadequate. When A Company staged a dawn raid on Kwangungsong, they found the birds had flown.

C Company pushed on to Tosan, where North Koreans had been seen digging in, but the lead carrier hit a mine and three men were seriously wounded. Lieutenant Weaver, though appearing unhurt, collapsed later in the day due to a fractured rib. They then came under heavy rife and machine-gun fire from front and rear as they climbed a hill. In all, two were killed and eight wounded, though the North Koreans suffered more than thirty dead.

Two companies of Northumberland Fusiliers came up from Kaesong to relieve the Glosters, who moved on by train and truck to the North Korean capital Pyongyang, then over the sweeping Taedong River into the pine forests of the north. Late in the afternoon of 30 November, they stopped in a pleasant green valley, flanked by rolling hills. There, Colonel Carne informed his company commanders that they were to do a real soldier's job at last. They were to stop the advance of the vast Chinese army as it headed south. The following day they began building defensive positions. But they saw no Chinese – only Americans in full retreat.

On 2 December, orders came to withdraw southwards. They were not to wait for the Chinese. The Americans had left already and the 29th Brigade had been left as a rearguard. Suddenly, the Glosters realised that they were all alone. Not only that, but their transport and not arrived. It was nearly dark and Colonel Carne began to march his battalion south as the snow began to fall.

The retreat was broken occasionally by a mug of hot tea and an opportunity for a sleep huddled together under blankets on frozen paddy fields. By 5 December, all the American troops were south of the Taedong River, heading for the next defensive line, leaving the British marching through a snowstorm as their rearguard. Eventually, the British reached the Taedong too; the Glosters were the last to cross. Colonel Carne then ordered the bridges blown, before they took off in American trucks through the burning ruins of Pyongyang, heading south to the small town of Sinmak, some 30 miles north of the 38th parallel. There they concentrated before moving off to dig defensive positions above the village of Chongsoktu'ri, which would mark the western end of the UN line.

Again before firing a shot in anger – or seeing a Chinese or North Korean soldier – they were ordered to withdraw. The British were now so used to the American's precipitate withdrawals – or 'bug-out fever' as it was known – that they began to ask, 'What will happen to us when the Americans leave the country?'

On 11 December, the Glosters were the last battalion to cross the 38th parallel and, just seventeen days after they had left, they found themselves back at Kaesong. It was here – not at home – that the Glosters would spend Christmas. This passed without incident, despite the potent Caribbean-style cocktail made from gin, whisky, rum, American-issue orange juice, American fruit cocktail, local hooch and evaporated milk supplied by Lieutenant Norrish and Sergeant Claxton. Then, early in the morning of 1 January 1951, the Chinese crossed the Imjin River and fell upon the 1st Republic of Korea Infantry Division.

The alarm was sounded at 0545 and the Glosters had moved forward by 1000. Colonel Carne went ahead and laid out a defensive position, which the battalion moved into by nightfall. There was a lull the next day, then on 3 January two enemy battalions attacked the Northumberland Fusiliers and the Royal Ulster Rifles. The 29th Brigade held the line, while the rest of the corps withdrew. All alone, the British put up a hell of a fight. By mid-afternoon the Chinese were routed, leaving heaps of dead on the battlefield. Mortars and artillery pummelled them as they fled.

Although the Glosters had held the middle of the line, they had had no contact with the Chinese. That evening they withdrew as the brigade was ordered to pull back through the South Korean capital Seoul and across the frozen Han River. They spent one night back in Suwon, then moved back to a new defensive position near the village of Pyongtaek 20 miles to the south.

From there the UN forces began to counterattack. They had a new commander, Lieutenant General Mathew Ridgeway, who put heart back into the US forces. He never appeared anywhere without two primed hand grenades strapped to his chest, earning him the nickname 'Iron Tits'.

The Glosters joined in the sorties to the north. Suwon was retaken. Then, at the end of January, the Glosters moved up to

Osan'ni as reserve for the attacking corps. It was cold and boring, sitting around waiting for action.

On 11 February, they moved up to Pabalmak. The following day they relieved an American cavalry battalion on a hill they had taken only the previous day. From there, the Glosters could see the Americans attacking Hill 350. Shortly after midnight, an enemy patrol penetrated Lieutenant Maycock's platoon area and were repulsed. Lieutenant Preston's position was raked with fire from close quarters, wounding Lieutenant Preston and two others. Preston had been on the phone to Major Angier when the call had to be abruptly terminated.

'I'm afraid I'll have to ring off now,' said Preston. 'They're about ten yards away.'

Corporal Armstrong's section held their fire until the approaching Chinese were at point-blank range, then opened up. A fire fight developed until heavy artillery and mortar fire drove off the Chinese. The following morning eleven bodies were found on the battlefield, some just 10 yards from Corporal Armstrong's slit trenches.

The battalion then advanced 3,000 yards towards the Han River. Before them, around 400 yards away, was Hill 327, codenamed 'Gloucester'. On it were a strong force of Chinese, well concealed and deeply dug in. On 13 February, Colonel Carne received orders to take it. But, before that, the Chinese counterattacked. Though their target was the 5th Cavalry Regiment to the right of the Glosters, some of their mortar fire fell on the Glosters' trenches. The following day the Cavalry were relieved by another brigade, who had orders to attack a feature called 'Cheltenham' to the right of Hill 327, thirty minutes before the Glosters crossed their start line.

At 1030 on 16 February, C Company under Major Walwyn and D Company under Major Wood moved forward to the start line. From there, the two columns picked their way slowly up the steep slope, which was covered with dwarf oaks, up to the 200-metre (218-yard) contour line, where they would begin the final assault. To the right, the Americans were making slow progress under heavy fire, some of which fell on the right flank of C Company. But the Chinese on Hill 327 still had not given away their position.

Artillery and tanks pummelled the hill, while mortars rained down any enemy positions on the reverse slope. Suddenly, grenades showered down on the Glosters, followed by rifle and machine-gun fire. Major Walwyn was wounded, and command of C Company was handed to Lieutenant Ware, a national-service officer, then to Captain Mardell.

Colonel Carne then ordered D Company to move round the left flank and attack up another spur. Lieutenant Simcox was shot dead hurling a grenade at a bunker, but the advance continued until the two sections of D Company reunited on the western edge of Hill 327.

C Company now attacked the bunkers in their sector, finding that the occupants still would not surrender when British weapons were actually in the bunker's mouths. One by one the bunkers had to be eliminated with small arms, bayonets and grenades as they moved along the narrow ridge.

By mid-afternoon, Gloucester had been secured and D

Company moved on to their next objective, only to find that the enemy had already abandoned it. The action had cost nine dead and twenty-seven wounded. Captain Mardell was awarded the Military Cross and Sergeant Eames the Military Medal in what had been the Glosters' first major battle.

The next day the advance continued. By the morning of the 18th, the battalion had moved forward 6,000 yards without further contact. Then, rounding a bend in the road, they found themselves overlooking the river. Brigadier Tom Brodies – known as 'Hopalong Cassidy' to the troops – wrote to the Colonel of the Regiment, Major-General Firth.

The Glosters, you will be glad to hear, had their big day two days ago when they captured an enormous hill, precipitous beyond words and the mere physical effort of climbing it was bad enough.

Fred Carne and his chaps did a wonderful show, starting at 10 am and finishing at tea-time, plain honest slogging up the hill, then the struggle for the top. They lost eight killed and about 30 wounded, and it might have been much worse. Charles Walwyn stopped one in the arm early on but I hope is OK. Young Mardell took over and was first class. We are all delighted as the Glosters had not had a real do before, but they certainly are on top of their form now.

Today we have as a result pushed right up to the river with little opposition, through the most terrific country I've yet met, hills for miles. We have been using 100 porters per battalion to supply and carry loads, and one company in addition, and striking right across country into the blue. Always in artillery range, luckily. It is an amazing war – jets, napalm, porters and load-carrying bullocks all in a brigade area at the same time.

After a short rest, the battalion moved back into the battle line on 21 March 1951 and were about to face one of the most glorious and annihilating battles in the regiment's history, one that would win them two Victoria Crosses and one George Cross. In the meantime, while the Glosters were resting up in a succession of dreary and devastated villages, the Americans had retaken Seoul on 14 March. On 3 April, they recrossed the 38th parallel and established the 'Kansas Line'. At the beginning of April, the Glosters moved up to the Kansas Line, occupying the towering hills along the south of the Imjin River. However, there were so few troops to hold this 8-mile front that the nearest ROK unit to the left was 3 miles away, while the 5th Northumberland Fusiliers were 2 miles to the right.

The Glosters were to deny the enemy the use of the road running south to Seoul. They relieved the Philippines Expeditionary Force, who had been in position for only a couple of days and had little intelligence about the enemy positions and strengths. Colonel Carne decided that he had better do something about that by sending frequent patrols across the Imjin, though they encountered no Chinese.

Carne then deployed his men in a classic defensive formation. A Company under Major Angier were moved forward to the left to the site of an old castle on Hill 148 west of the village of

Choksong. D Company under Major Wood were on a hill to the southeast of the village, while B Company under Major Harding guarded the right flank to the east. Headquarters was established at the point where the road running south entered the hills and crossed a shallow stream. C Company under Major Mitchell were held in reserve on the high ground directly above, with their backs to the towering mountain Kamak-San. The mouth of the open valley that ran towards the river was held by the Drums. This was overlooked by the triangular-shaped Hill 235 to the west, which was occupied by the assault pioneers under Captain Pike.

This formation created a front 7 miles wide and 5 miles deep. Any approaching enemy would have to fight their way through at least two companies of riflemen and two sections of Vickers machine guns. These would be supported by the Glosters' 3-inch mortar platoon, the mortars of C Troop, 170 Mortar Battery, the guns of 45 Field Artillery Regiment and, hopefully, the artillery of the US 3rd Division.

The problem with such a widely spread formation was that the enemy might infiltrate at night. However, after eight days, a truckload of barbed wire turned up. The second truckload did not arrive until eleven days later, when the situation had changed substantially.

Colonel Carne's patrols had established that the ford carrying the road from Seoul northward was intact and that the enemy defensive positions on the far bank were empty. However, on the high ground above they could see movement among the bunkers to the north. A and D Companies were sent in at night to sweep these bunkers, but found that they had been abandoned. Eager to find out where the enemy had gone, Colonel Carne ordered six major sweeps across the river. He personally led one by day and one by night. His second-in-command, Major Digby Grist, followed with a third daylight sortie. A fourth was supported by an armoured squadron of the 8th Hussar. Eventually, when they reached 7 miles beyond the Imjin, they came across a handful of half-starved Chinese soldiers, whom they captured. This was the rearguard of the Red Army. They were ill-equipped and poorly clad, and had little knowledge of the whereabouts of their units. They had simply been told to watch enemy troop movements and wait for their comrades to return to begin a new offensive.

Although the Chinese were in full retreat, Ridgway was in no position to pursue them. Having replaced General MacArthur on 11 April, he had been ordered not to thrust deep into North Korea as the UN forces had the previous year. He was to hold the 38th parallel, the old demarcation like between North and South. At the west, this ran roughly along the line of the Imjin River.

The problem with this strategy was that it allowed the Chinese to regroup in safety inside North Korea. Now, with the winter over, resupplied and replenished, the Chinese went on the offensive again. On 13 April small reconnaissance parties began moving south at night, infiltrating the UN positions. During the day they rested up and kept watch on the UN troops movements.

On 21 April the main force followed. Among them were the 63rd Army, who were made up of three divisions: the 187th, the 188th and the 189th. Their orders were to open up the ancient route to Seoul, which ran straight through the Glosters' position.

Early in the afternoon of 22 April, the Glosters' artillery post saw twenty enemy soldiers in dark uniforms patrolling the opposite bank. A larger body of men, perhaps as many as a hundred, were moving behind a hill directly north of the ford now known as Gloster Crossing. Air reconnaissance found five more parties between ten and twenty strong reoccupying their old position on the north bank and directed artillery fire on them.

Surveying the scene, Colonel Carne wondered whether this might be a feint, but soon realised that it was the build-up to an all-out attack. He gave orders for the Glosters to lie low and keep their positions concealed. It was clear to Colonel Carne that the Chinese were planning to send a party across the river that night. A Company's observation post was to watch the ford until dusk, mortaring and shelling any attempt to cross during daylight. Then, at nightfall, C Company were to sent No. 7 Platoon under Lieutenant Guy Temple, son of Major-General Bertie Temple of the regiment, to lie in ambush on the south side of the crossing.

For the rest of the day, the Glosters rested, ate a hot meal and checked their weapons and ammunition, and half the reserve ammunition was brought up to the headquarters site. As dusk fell, Lieutenant Temple and his men slipped down from the hills and took up their position at the end of the ford. Then they waited.

The attack did not come immediately. When it did, it came in greater force than was expected. That evening air reconnaissance had seen only small enemy formations approaching the river. The main body was then still 12 miles away. But, in a forced march carrying full battle gear, the Chinese reached the Imjin in three hours.

Lieutenant Temple's platoon waited in the moonlight. Then, after an hour or so, they heard a splash and Chinese in parties of three and four began crossing the river. Soon the Imjin seemed to be full of Chinese, all clearly illuminated by the moon. Temple's men held their fire until the Chinese were almost upon them. Then they opened up, killing at least thirty of them in thirty seconds and sending the others racing for the other shore. But they would soon be back, this time not in dozens, but in hundreds.

Under continuous small-arms and mortar fire, the Chinese made four attempts to cross the Imjin, losing so many men that the river became choked with the dead, wounded and drowning. Every man in Temple's platoon had killed at least three. Private Allen, who had performed indifferently at the range in Colchester, counted ten corpses in front of his position. Not a single Gloster was killed or wounded and Lieutenant Temple was awarded the Military Cross for this action.

However, ammunition was soon running low and it became apparent that they could not hold back the sheer weight of numbers being thrown against them. After the fourth attempt to cross the river had been beaten back, Temple realised that the next would swamp them and, with five minutes' ammunition left, his men pulled back under artillery cover. However, the Chinese plan to force their way swiftly through the battalion's front, forcing its withdrawal, cut off the entire UN left wing and open the road to Seoul, had been disrupted.

Unbeknown to the Glosters, there was another crossing point. A mile and a half away downstream, there was an ancient under-water bridge, not marked on any map, that led across to a sand spit. Thousands of Chinese poured across and attacked A Company at the old castle, outnumbering them six to one, while a third thrust across the road to the east attack D Company.

Upstream, the company of 5th Fusiliers on the left flank holding a ridge overlooking the river were forced to withdraw. This allowed the Chinese battalion that had been attacking them to move south and attack B Company of the Glosters. So, by midnight, the three forward rifle companies of the Glosters were all in action.

Barely half an hour into the battle, Colonel Carne began to receive alarming reports from his forward companies. They talked of continuous attacks by overwhelming numbers, requests for more mortar and artillery support, and mounting casualties. Over and over came the same refrain: 'They're coming again.' Imperturbable, Fred Carne continued smoking his slow-burning pipe. He remained calm and never raised his voice. But no one in headquarters got any sleep that night.

A Company hurled back one assault after another, while B Company fended off probing attacks, with considerable loss to the Chinese. One party attacking Corporal Crisp's sector were wiped out with grenades. Private Robson accounted for thirteen with his Bren gun, while No. 6 Platoon counted thirty bodies in front of their position. Suffering no loss themselves,

B Company had killed at least a hundred enemy before the sun came up.

The Chinese had attacked along the entire UN line. The UN's superior firepower did considerable damage to the advancing Chinese, but at a distance from which artillery could not engage the targets adequately. The Kansas Line was so spread out that it soon consisted of a series of strong points, each of which would have to hold out for the entire line to hold. Their only hope was air cover. But for that they would have to wait until morning.

Before dawn on the 23rd, the battalion command post was moved up to a bunker on the ridge held by C Company. From there Colonel Carne could see for himself the attacks on the hills to the north.

Although A Company had inflicted huge casualties on the enemy, half their number were dead or wounded and the rest were exhausted from the night's fighting. Second-Lieutenant John Maycock had been killed and his platoon, who had been holding the site of the old castle, were reduced to six unwounded men. They had been withdrawn before they were wiped out. The remains had been assigned to Lieutenant Philip Curtis's platoon, which was also, now, considerably under strength.

Up until that point, A Company had not lost the highest point of their position. But the Chinese pushed them back. They set up machine-gun posts there and sprayed bullets over the defenders. Just after dawn on the 23rd, Major Angier told the adjutant, Captain Anthony Farrar-Hockley, who went on to became the official historian of the Korean War and commander-in-chief of NATO, 'I'm afraid we've lost Castle Site.

I'm mounting a counterattack now, but I want to know whether to expect to stay here indefinitely or not. If I am staying on, I must be reinforced as my numbers are getting very low.'

The message was passed to Colonel Carne, who considered the situation. He wondered whether the Chinese would continue their attack in daylight, once UN aircraft were aloft. He also wondered how long it would be before the Chinese realised that his battalion's flanks were open and completely encircle him.

After a brief conversation with Angier, Carne told him, 'You will stay there until further notice.' A Company's position still overlooked the river-crossing points and the approaches to D Company's position. If they withdrew, the Chinese could freely reinforce their troops on the south bank and swamp D Company and then B Company. Ammunition was sent to A Company, but reinforcements were out of the question.

'Don't worry about us,' said Major Angier. 'We'll be all right.'

'Good luck,' Farrar-Hockley replied.

A quarter of an hour later Major Angier would be dead.

As long as the Chinese remained on Castle Site, A Company would suffer more casualties. Their machine guns there would rain down fire on No. 2 Platoon under Lieutenant Terence Waters, as well as Lieutenant Curtis's No. 1 Platoon. Unless Castle Site was retaken, the Chinese could reinforce their position for a further advance that would push the Glosters off the hill altogether.

Under the guns of 70 Field Battery, Lieutenant Curtis led his platoon in a counterattack. However, the Chinese machine-gun post was occupying a bunker on the top of Castle Site that had overhead protection to protect it from artillery fire and continued to harry the advancing Glosters with heavy fire. The final thrust had to be made over open ground with no cover. Three men fell dead by the time they had advanced 20 yards. A minute later four more were wounded. After some initial success, the advance stalled under heavy fire. Enemy from just below the crest of the hill were rushed to reinforce the position and a fierce fire fight developed, with grenades also being used freely by both sides in this close-quarter engagement.

Lieutenant Curtis ordered some of his men to give him covering fire while he himself rushed the main position of resistance. Gathering a group of men, Curtis worked his way under intense fire to a dip in the ground only 20 yards from the bunker. The machine gun and the gunners were clearly visible through the aperture. Curtis began to hurl bunker grenades handed to him by his men. The Chinese returned heavy fire, forcing all but Curtis to retreat.

Then, Lieutenant Curtis was severely wounded in the head by shrapnel from a grenade. Several of his men crawled out and pulled him back under cover. Corporal Papworth of the Royal Army Medical Corps began to tend to the wounded, but Lieutenant Curtis would not wait.

'We must take the Castle Site,' he said.

'Just wait until Papworth has seen you,' said the soldier by his side.

Recovering slightly, Lieutenant Curtis insisted on making a second attempt. Roughly bandaged, he struggled to get up but was held down by his men, one of whom sat on his chest to restrain him. Despite this, Curtis managed to break free and made another desperate charge, clearly in pain, with pistol and grenade in hand. Possibly waiting until the single advancing figure was at point-blank range, the Chinese machine-gunners held their fire. Staggering to within a few yards of the bunker, Curtis pulled the pin on the grenade and threw it. As it flew through the air, the Chinese machine-gunners opened up, killing him with a burst of fire just a few yards from his objective. Moments later they, too, were dead. The grenade landed in the bunker opening, blowing away the muzzle of the gun and killing those inside.

Not far away, Major Angier was leading another assault, where he was killed. Command passed to the only surviving officer, Lieutenant Waters. However, by the time he had arrived to take over, the opportunity to retake the Castle Site had gone. But Curtis's sacrifice was not in vain.

According to the citation on this Victoria Cross, awarded on 1 December 1953:

Although the immediate objective of this counter-attack was not achieved, it had yet a great effect on the subsequent course of the battle; for although the enemy had gained a footing on a position vital to the defence of the whole company area, this success had resulted in such furious reaction that they made no further effort to exploit their success in this immediate area; had they done so, the eventual withdrawal of the company might well have proved impossible.

It concluded, 'Lieutenant Curtis's conduct was magnificent throughout this bitter battle.'

Although the record of Lieutenant Philip Curtis's achievement is now secure in the annals of the Gloucester Regiment, he did not belong to it. Born in Devonport in 1926, he had first seen action during World War Two at the age of fourteen as a messenger for the ARP wardens in the Plymouth blitz. Later, he volunteered for the RAF, but was told to come back in eighteen months because he was too young. Instead, he joined the army and served in the ranks from September 1944 to May 1946, without seeing any action overseas. Then he was given an emergency commission in the Duke of Cornwall's Light Infantry. Discharged in 1948, he remained in the reserve while finding employment at Roneo, the duplicator firm. But he found civilian life exceedingly dull.

Then disaster struck. His young wife died, leaving him with a baby daughter. Soon after, he received his recall papers. Having a small child, he could have claimed exemption. But his mother-in-law took in the child and he rejoined the army in September 1950. In March 1951, he was seconded into the Glosters.

Since the Chinese eventually overran the Glosters who then spent the rest of the war in a prisoner-of-war camp, there was no one to recommend Lieutenant Curtis for a decoration until their return at the end of the war. The Victoria Cross was awarded to Lieutenant Curtis posthumously on 1 December 1953 and the investiture took place on 6 July 1954. His mother, mother-in-law and seven-year-old daughter Susan attended to accept the award. Lieutenant Curtis is buried at the Commonwealth War Graves cemetery in Korea.

With A Company unable to retake Castle Hill, there was little they could do to help D Company, who were also suffering a ferocious onslaught. What's more their commander, Major 'Lakri' Wood was on leave in Japan. Hearing of the Chinese offensive, he tried to get back to Korea, but, despite pestering every airfield in Japan, he could not get air transport. So in command was Captain Mike Harvey, formerly of the Royal Hampshire Regiment, who was a black belt in Judo.

Colonel Carne received orders to hold the road between Choksong and Solma-ri. But it became clear to Carne that neither A nor D Company could hold its position without air support. At around 0900, airstrikes had forced the Chinese to withdraw further up the line, but none were available to relieve the pressure on the Glosters. The brigade commander had already given his permission for Carne to withdraw his forward positions and when, fifty minutes later, it was clear that no air support would be forthcoming, Carne gave orders for A and D Companies to withdraw to positions just northwest and west of battalion headquarters and B Company on a hill under the towering Kamak-San.

As the two companies broke away from the enemy, the whole firepower of the battalion – the heavy-mortar troops and three batteries of 45 Field Regiment – was used against the 187th Division in their positions in the hilltops. The positions that the Glosters had relinquished were soon full of Chinese dead.

Meanwhile, the wounded were being helicoptered out and the chaplain, Sam Davies, was conducting a funeral service for

Major Angier, whose body had been brought back to headquarters in one of the Oxford carriers used for transporting ammunition. The second-in-command, Major Digby Grist, came forward to see if he could be of any assistance. But soon after he arrived news came that the battalion's rear headquarters was under attack.

'I think you'd better go back at once, Digby, to see what's happening,' said Colonel Carne.

Grist set off calmly with his driver, Bainbridge. Half an hour later, they were running the gauntlet of a Chinese ambush.

While A and D Companies were withdrawing, B Company on the right flank withdrew secretly to new positions as yet unknown to the enemy. When Chinese patrols were spotted in the vicinity, Sergeant Petherick was sent out to lay an ambush. Soon afterwards, two hundred Chinese from the 188th Division walked into it and a fire fight began. When the Chinese began to outflank them, Petherick withdrew, but other elements went forward under the cover of medium and heavy mortar fire. There began a series of minor engagements among the knolls that lay at the foot of Kamak-San to keep the Chinese off their main position. Then, as twilight fell, the 188th withdrew.

The Chinese commander-in-chief, Peng The-Huai, was far from happy with the performance of the 63rd Army. The 187th Division should have smashed through the Glosters the previous night and the 188th Division should, by now, be marching down the Seoul road to cut behind the British 29th Brigade and the 3rd United States Army, who were fighting to the northeast. But it was not too late to catch them. If they could dispose of the

Glosters early on the night of the 23rd, they could still make a forced march down the road to Uijongbu.

Just before midnight, Major Harding reported, 'Well, we've started. They're attacking Beverley's platoon now – about a hundred and fifty, I should think.'

An artillery forward-observation officer directing covering fire for C Company reported the same thing. The 188th were trying to force the right flank of the battalion and take the commanding heights of Kamak-San.

B and C Companies came under wave after wave of attack. Ranks of screaming Chinese attacked with rifles, sub-machine-guns and grenades, under the cover of heavy machine guns and mortar fire. They were repulsed with small-arms, heavy-mortar and artillery fire.

Early on, the Chinese were at a disadvantage. Major Harding's move meant that the enemy did not know where they were and had to stumble on blindly, often suffering enfilading fire. Then, sometime after 0200 on the 24th, a new regiment were brought up who had a clearer idea where B Company were, and at 0245 a new onslaught began.

At 0300, the commander of C Company, Major Mitchell, reported, 'I'm afraid they've overrun my top position and they're reinforcing hard. They're simply pouring chaps in above us. Let me know what the colonel wants me to do.'

Colonel Carne knew what he had to do. With the ridge overlooking C Company in enemy hands and the overwhelming odds, the right half of the battalion had been split wide open. Below were the artillery, the mortars, the regimental first-aid point, the wounded and the headquarters with its radio links to the battalion command post and the brigade headquarters.

'Pack the headquarters up,' he said. 'Get everyone out of the valley up between D Company and the anti-tank platoon in position. I'm going to withdraw C Company in ten minutes, and I shall move B over to join us in the morning.'

Pulling C Company out during the hours of darkness was an extremely difficult operation and only a third of the men made it to the final position on Hill 235.

Meanwhile B Company repulsed no fewer than seven all-out attacks and the forward sections were overwhelmed by sheer weight of numbers. By dawn on the 24th, they had practically run out of ammunition. When the grenades ran out, men hurled beer bottles at the oncoming Chinese. On every company front, men were now embroiled in bitter hand-to-hand fighting with bayonets, rifle butts, entrenching tools, boots and bare knuckles.

Disengaging B Company was also going to cause a problem as the fighting continued. But fortunately the Chinese commander concentrated all his strength on one platoon – that of Lieutenant Costello, who held firm with the wounded fighting alongside their unscathed comrades. Shell fire and bursts from Sergeant Sykes's Vickers machine guns held the Chinese back, while Major Harding withdrew the rest of the company, with Lieutenant Peal's platoon as rearguard. As they reached the foot of Hill 235, the formation of Chinese following them closed in, but they were driven off by Private Walker of C Company, who, on his own initiative, ran down the hill firing his Bren gun from the hip.

Only twenty men of B Company survived the withdrawal. They were combined with the remnants of C Company under the command of Major Harding. Together they amounted to about one weak platoon. And their position was far from secure. Before they arrived, Colonel Carne had come across a group of Chinese infiltrating. With the aid of his driver and two regimental policemen, he forced them back with bayonets and grenades, killing two of them.

'What was all that about?' asked Captain Farrar-Hockley when Carne came back over the ridge.

'Oh, just shooing away some Chinese,' said Carne.

With all the Glosters together now on Hill 235 – now renamed Glosters' Hill – the battalion's front line had shrunk from 8 to 4 miles, then to 600 yards – but still it had not been breached at any point. They were now some 300-men strong, including drivers, cooks, pioneers, medical orderlies and signallers. As Colonel Carne observed to Captain Farrar-Hockley, 'It seems to me that you and I are going to find a job for ourselves as riflemen before very much longer.'

Colonel Carne's first task now was the organisation of the hill's defences. He made a tour of inspection between 0700 and 0845 in the weak morning sun and a detachment was organised to scramble down the steep path to headquarters and collect ammunition and any other supplies that were left behind. A message came that the Philippines Expeditionary Force headed by armour and infantry in brigade strength were on their way to relieve them. By the evening of the following day, they should be back in reserve. All they had to do was hold on.

But as the day drew on the bad news came through. The relief column had been held up by the Chinese, who were holding the southern end of hill road. Tanks of the 8th Hussars had gone to force their way through, but the lead tanks had been ambushed and the road was now blocked with the burned-out vehicles. What was more, now that the Chinese had bypassed the Glosters, the entire 29th Brigade and the 3rd Division had been cut off. The relief column was certainly not going to reach them that day, said Brigadier Brodie, but it was essential for the Glosters to hold their position.

'I understand the position quite clearly,' said Colonel Carne, studying the map. 'What I must make clear is that my command is no longer an effective fighting force. If it's required that we shall stay here in spite of this, we shall continue to hold. But I wish to make known the nature of my position.'

But Brodie had no choice. The Royal Northumberland Fusiliers and the Belgian Battalion had already come under violent attack and by the dawn of the 25th Brodie realised that with all units fighting defensive actions there was no chance of mounting a counterattack. He must withdraw his brigade. Although they had already suffered a severe mauling, the Belgians were withdrawn with comparative ease. Next to go were the 5th Fusiliers and the Royal Ulster Rifles. But there was only one order he could give the Glosters: 'Hold on where you are.'

Not only that, but they must go on the attack. It was vital that they pose a threat to the Chinese so that they would be forced to retain forces near to the Imjin rather than leave them free rein to attack the forces retreating to the south.

Carne's position was impossible, on paper at least. He had just three hundred men, enough ammunition for just twelve hours' fighting and supplies of food and water running desperately low. On the bare rocky hillside, it was impossible to dig in, but rock sangars were built to afford some protection. And morale was still high. When a mortarman was told that they were to make their last stand on Glosters' Hill, he said, 'Us'll be all right, sir – t'will be like the Rock of Gibraltar.'

The worst problem was the one hundred wounded, seventy of them stretcher cases. Private Bounden drove down the bullet-swept road in the medical officer's jeep, fitted with a stretcher, searching for more. They were attended by the medical officer Captain Bob Hickley, his assistant Sergeant 'Knocker' Brisland and two men from the Royal Army Medical Corps – Sergeant Baxter and Corporal Papworth. However, the wounded lay out in the open, where they were regularly swept with machine-gun fire, often wounding them again. The chaplain, Sam Davies, was constantly on hand to give succour to the living, comfort the dying and bury the dead.

An American helicopter tried to evacuate some of the wounded, but could not land due to the intensity of the fire. An airdrop of vital blood plasma hit the spot, but other precious supplies fell on the lower slopes of the hill, where they could not be reached. Further attempts to break through by the Americans, Belgians, Puerto Ricans, Filipinos and 8th Hussar reached no further that a thousand yards from Hill 235. The Glosters were inextricably cut off. And still the Chinese kept coming on. Despite mortars and the 45th Field Regiment's 25-pounders, which were firing more rounds per weapon than at El Alamein, the Chinese numbers were swelling.

By the night of the 24th, the 188th Division had lost more than four thousand men since it had crossed the Imjin. Now the 189th crossed the river with orders to clear away the Glosters once and for all. They had had all day to study the lie of the land and plan their night attack. As soon as it was dark, six companies advanced from their assembly point behind Castle Hill and slowly began to ascend the hill, aiming to get within 25 yards of the defenders before they began hurling grenades. But the tripwires and tin cans the Glosters had put out alerted them. At around 2045, 45 Field Regiment opened up again on the densely pack ranks of the enemy. Nevertheless, several hundred Chinese got through the Glosters' defences. They blew bugles and whistles discordantly to disorient their dogged foes. But by 2300 they had been driven back.

The Glosters sent their wounded back to Captain Hickley's makeshift field hospital and laid their dead in hollows. Three hours later, the Chinese renewed their onslaught. In fierce exchanges of grenades and rifle and machine-gun fire, the battle swayed back and forth. Then, towards dawn, thousands more Chinese began their ascent of the hill from the east, directed, once again, by bugles so off-key that Drum-Major Buss winced every time he heard one.

'It will be a long time before I want to hear a cavalry trumpet playing after this,' said Colonel Carne.

'It would serve them right, sir, if we confused them by playing our own bugles,' said Captain Farrar-Hockley. 'I wonder which direction they would go if they heard "Defaulters".'

'Have we got a bugle up here?' said Carne.

Farrar-Hockley called down to Drum-Major Buss, who said he had one in his haversack.

'Well, play it, drum-major,' said Farrar-Hockley.

'What shall it be, sir?' asked the drum-major.

'It's getting near daylight. Play "Reveille" – the long and the short,' said Farrar-Hockley. 'And play "Fire" call – in fact, play all the calls of the day as far as "Retreat", but don't play that.'

Buss played the long and the short 'Reveille', 'Defaulters', 'Cookhouse', 'Orderly Room', 'Orderly NCOs', 'Officers Dress for Dinner', 'Lights Out' and the 'Last Post', along with the American version of 'Reveille' and 'Taps', with the men cheering the drum-major on.

'He always played the bugle well,' recalled Farrar-Hockley, 'and that day he was not below form. The sweet notes of our own bugle, which now echoed through the valley below him, died away. For a moment there was silence – the last note had coincided with a lull in the action. Then the noise of battle began again – but with a difference: there was no sound of a Chinese bugle. There are not many drum-majors in the British Army who can claim to have silenced the enemy's battle calls with a short bugle recital.'

Drum-Major Buss's bugle playing temporarily confused the enemy. Perhaps fearing a counterattack, they ceased any movement for a while. But, after dawn, fresh waves of the enemy attacked. To the north A Company were driven back from their position. All that remained of them were one officer, CSM Gallagher, and 27 men.

The headquarters had practically ceased to exist. Signals officer Captain Richard Reeve-Tucker was dead. The assistant adjutant, Lieutenant Donald Allman, was commanding the remnants of a platoon, despite a painful shoulder wound. The intelligence officer, Lieutenant Henry Cabral, was commanding another. Captain Farrar-Hockley, winner of the Military Cross in World War Two, now found the position of adjutant redundant. There was no point in relaying orders to officers who were fighting for their lives or sitting by a radio whose batteries were failing, waiting for messages that never came. He seized the opportunity for action. With Sergeants Clayden and Tuggey and Privates Masters, Middleton and Guilding, he led a bayonet charge that forced the Chinese back and restored A Company to its original position, with the help of 45 Field Regiment, who bombarded the Chinese as they renewed the assault.

Ejected, the Chinese massed again. The company's forward observation officer, Captain Washbrook, then called a series of airstrikes, blanketing the north slopes with napalm. The defenders cheered when they saw six more F80s attack concentrations of enemy troops between Glosters' Hill and the river. Finally, at 0630 on the morning of 25 April, the Chinese pulled back. Suddenly there was cause for optimism. The Glosters had made it through the night. They soon expected an airdrop of supplies and the sight of the relief column rolling in. But then the transports flying overhead did not turn for their run-in for a supply drop, but headed out to sea. Then Farrar-Hockley received a call to say that he was wanted back at headquarters.

Colonel Carne was sitting by the rear-link radio. He got up when Farrar-Hockley arrived.

'You know that armoured-infantry column that's coming up from 3 Division to relieve us?' he said.

'Yes, sir,' said Farrar-Hockley.

'Well, it isn't coming.'

'Right, sir.'

There did not seem to be much more to be said, recalled Farrar-Hockley.

The Chinese were pushing so hard from the east that the relief column intended for the Glosters was needed to cover the withdrawal of the division to Uijongbu. There were no troops available to fight their way forward to the Glosters. They were to fight their way back on their own.

There was a last distribution of ammunition to those still fit enough to bear arms. Each rifleman got five rounds, each Bren gunner one and a half magazines, each Sten gunner half a magazine. That was all they had left.

At 0730, a message was sent back to brigade headquarters saying that the wireless batteries would last only another half an hour. Under this message in the brigade log, Brigadier Brodie wrote, 'Nobody but the Glosters could have done it.'

Then Colonel Carne accompanied his remaining officers over to the edge of the ridge to point out the route they would be taking. Then he turned to Captain Hickley and said, 'Bob, I'm afraid we shall have to leave the wounded behind.'

'Very well, sir,' said Captain Hickley after a pause. 'I quite understand the position.'

The breakout was planned for 1000. Colonel Carne explained that the companies would break out independently in the hope that some of them would make it back to the UN line to the south. There would be no relief column, no more airstrikes and no more artillery support, since the 45th Field Regiment were under heavy attack themselves.

For breakfast on the morning of 25 April there was tinned fruit and condensed milk for those who were lucky, nothing for those who were not. Then the Glosters destroyed anything that might be of use to the Chinese.

When it was time to withdraw from Glosters' Hill, there were just 169 men standing, but the Chinese had suffered such huge losses that they never again attempted a similar frontal assault. For the wounded Glosters there could be no escape. Captain Hickley, Sergeant Brisland and the chaplain all volunteered to stay behind to look after them. Then the remnants of the battalion moved off to the south and almost immediately found themselves under heavy machine-gun fire.

The remains of A Company under Captain Farrar-Hockley found themselves in a valley with Chinese machine guns on the hills to either side of the road.

'Light and heavy machine-guns fired towards us, yet they did not hit us,' he recalled in his memoir *The Edge of the Sword*.

There can be no doubt that, had they wished to, they could have mown us down like grass before a scythe. Exposed entirely to their weapons... the message they conveyed was quite plain: we are up here; you are down there; you are exposed; we are concealed and you are in our sights. As we moved on, the fire from three machine-guns came down again, this time a good deal lower – unmistakably lower. I knew there was but one course open to me if the men with me were to remain alive for more than five minutes.

Feeling that he had betrayed everything he loved and believed in, he ordered his men to halt and put their weapons down.

Moments later he heard Major Sam Weller, company commander of the support company, give the same order. Not far away Captain 'Spike' Pike and his party found themselves in the same situation. He loosed off two of the four rounds remaining in his pistol. But he reckoned that his men had only fifty rounds between them and they were outnumbered by at least ten to one. He, too, had no choice but to surrender.

Major Paul Mitchell, commanding C Company, had been out of touch with battalion headquarters for 48 hours and went to see what was going on. He found the area abandoned. Suddenly confronted by six Chinese soldiers, he made a dash for it and got away. He managed to link up with Captain Bill Bartlett and the anti-tank platoon. They ran into an ambush and most of the men were killed, wounded or captured. But Mitchell and Bartlett managed to get away.

Major Harding, Lieutenant Temple and CSM Ridlington reached a point 10 miles south before being captured. Lieutenant Henry Cabral headed off alone and found himself surrounded by the Chinese. He tried to hide up until nightfall, but was captured. He died in a prisoner-of-war camp after a year, having been continually castigated for adopting an 'incorrect attitude'.

The second-in-command, Major Digby Grist, left the rear headquarters and headed for the brigade in a jeep. He ran into an ambush and had his windscreen shot out. But his driver put his foot down and drove through the hail of bullets. Digby Grist arrived at brigade headquarters with a neat bullet hole in his right wrist.

A group under Captain Harvey took another approach. They headed north, then west. The journey was not without incident, but 46 of his men survived to reach UN lines.

Colonel Carne, together with RSM Hobbs and CSM Strong evaded capture for a day. But then he and his men were marched into captivity across the Imjin River, accompanied by the Chinese 63rd Army, which had been so badly mauled that it had to withdraw over the river to regroup.

In the prisoner-of-war camp, Colonel Carne and his men suffered appalling conditions. They were tortured and starved, and forced to work at backbreaking labour aimed to break their spirits, and listen to lectures that attempted to convert them to Communism. Again, Carne's steadfastness and resilience was an inspiration to others. At one stage he and a fellow officer were convicted of having a 'generally hostile' attitude to Communism. He was forced to read a bogus confession and was put in solitary confinement, where he preserved his sanity by making stone carvings.

Meanwhile, his battalion was awarded the US Presidential Citation for its action on the Imjin River. In a personal letter to the Glosters' new commanding officer, Lieutenant Colonel Grist, General Ridgway wrote:

1. Your unit has already been officially cited for its heroic stand at the Imjin River. However, as Commander-in-Chief, United Nations Command, I wish to add my personal commendation.
2. All members of the United Nations Force fought with distinction during that particular action but the indomitable spirit of the personnel of the 1st Battalion, the Gloucestershire Regiment was outstanding. Their refusal to withdraw prevented an early penetration of our lines and provided critically needed time for other units to regroup.
3. It is with great pride that I join all the freedom-loving peoples of the world in expressing admiration of their gallant stand.

Released after two years of captivity, Carne and his men returned to a heroes' welcome at Southampton on 15 October 1953. His only comment on his captivity was, 'I have gained a little pride in being British and have lost a little weight.'

Two weeks later, the Queen decorated Colonel Carne with the Victoria Cross at Buckingham Palace. The citation read:

On the night of 22–23 April 1951, Lieutenant-Colonel Carne's battalion, 1 Glosters, was heavily attacked and the enemy on the Imjin River were repulsed, having suffered heavy casualties. On 23, 24 and 25 April 1951, the Battalion was heavily and incessantly engaged by vastly superior numbers of enemy, who repeatedly launched mass attacks, but were stopped at close quarters.

During 24 and 25 April 1951, the Battalion was completely cut off from the rest of the Brigade, but remained a fighting entity, in face of almost continual onslaughts from an enemy who were determined, at all costs and regardless of casualties, to over-run it. Throughout, Lieutenant-Colonel Carne's manner remained coolness itself, and on the wireless, the only communication he still had with Brigade, he repeatedly assured the Brigade Commander that all was well with his Battalion, that they could hold on and that everyone was in good heart.

Throughout the entire engagement, Lieutenant-Colonel Carne, showing a complete disregard for his own safety, moved among the whole Battalion under very heavy mortar and machine-gun fire, inspiring the utmost confidence and the will to resist, amongst his troops. On two separate occasions, armed with a rifle and grenades, he personally led assault parties which drove back the enemy and saved important situations.

Lieutenant-Colonel Carne's example of courage, coolness and leadership was felt not only in his own Battalion, but throughout the whole Brigade. He fully realised that his flanks had been turned, but he also knew that the abandonment of his position would clear the way for the enemy to make a major break-through and this would have endangered the Corps. When at last it was apparent that his battalion would not be relieved and on orders from higher authority, he organised his battalion into small, officer-led parties, who then broke out, whilst he himself in charge of a small party fought his way out, but was captured within 24 hours.

Lieutenant-Colonel Carne showed powers of leadership which can seldom have been surpassed in the history of our Army. He inspired his officers and men to fight beyond the normal limits of human endurance, in spite of overwhelming odds and ever-increasing casualties, shortage of ammunition and of water.

On 21 November he led the 28th/61st for the last time as it marched through the streets of Gloucester. Peels of bells rang out from all the churches and a service of thanksgiving was held at the cathedral, where the Dean was assisted by Sam Davies, the chaplain on Glosters' Hill. During the service, a stone cross that Carne had carved using a two rusty nails and an improvised hammer during his nineteen months in solitary confinement was presented to the cathedral.

Everyone who had fought alongside Colonel Carne at Imjin said that he had carried them all with his courage. But, before Korea, his life had been anything but exceptional. Born in Falmouth in 1906, he was educated at the Imperial Service

College and the Royal Military College, Sandhurst. Commissioned in the Gloucester Regiment in 1925, he was seconded into the King's African rifles from 1930 to 1936. He returned to the Glosters as adjutant in 1937 but, with the outbreak of World War Two, he was sent back to the King's African rifles, serving on the staff in Madagascar. He commanded the 6th and 26th Battalions of the King's African rifles from 1943 to 1946, seeing action in Burma in 1944. Then he took command of the 5th Battalion of the Glosters when it reformed in 1947.

During twenty years of service, he had just four medal ribbons. Korea would give him five more. He earned the DSO for the attack on Hill 327 in February. He was known as a calm, quiet, almost inarticulate man who inspired the utmost confidence in his men. He had one piece of advice for fellow officers. In intelligence reports the enemy were referred to as 'guerrillas' or 'bandits'. It was best, he said, to remember that they were highly trained soldiers and arrangements should be made to deal with them accordingly.

During the defence of Hill 235, he never seemed to eat or sleep and showed complete disregard for his own safety. Armed with a rifle and bayonet, he personally led a number of attacks on the enemy. Except when engaged in hand-to-hand fighting with the enemy, he never swore or raised his voice, and he filled his command post with the soothing smell of navy cut tobacco burning slowly in his well-seasoned briar.

As well as the DSO and VC, Carne was also award the American Distinguished Service Cross. He was granted the freedom of Gloucester in 1953, an honour then shared with three other people: the Duke and Duchess of Gloucester and the Duke of Beaufort. He was given the freedom of Falmouth the following year. In 1957, he was present in Korea at the unveiling of a memorial on Glosters' Hill. Retiring from the army that year, he settled in Cranham, Gloucestershire, and became the deputy lieutenant for Gloucester in 1960.

Carne died of pneumonia and carcinoma of the pharynx at the Cotswold Nuffield Nursing Home on 19 April 1986, survived by his wife and stepson. He was buried in Cranham. The stone cross that he had carved for use at the PoW camp services remains in Gloucester Cathedral.

CHAPTER THREE

THE BEER-BOTTLE
VC

PRIVATE WILLIAM SPEAKMAN
4 November 1951, Black Watch (Royal Highland Regiment), attached to
1st Battalion King's Own Scottish Borderers

In April 1951, the 1st King's Own Scottish Borderers was sent from
Hong Kong to join the United Nation forces in Korea. It arrived
at Inchon on 23 April, while the Glorious Glosters were winning
their VCs at the Battle of Imjin River. The Borderers went into
action immediately they reached the front. They had barely got
stuck in when they were ordered to withdraw, along with the rest
of United Nations force, leaving the Glosters stranded.

The Borderers were part of the Commonwealth Division,
which re-established a position back along the 38th Parallel on
the Imjin River, once the Chinese advance had been halted and
reversed. In late September, a new advance was ordered by the

United Nations and on 3 October, the King's Own Scottish Borderers joined battle to take possession of Hill 355. A new defensive line was set up there, but it came under frequent attack for the rest of October.

On 4 November, the Chinese launched six thousand men in an all-out attack on a vital two-hill ridgeline position on the 1st Commonwealth Division's front. The British troops called this 'Charlie Chinaman's Gunpowder Plot' because it came on the eve of Guy Fawkes Night. The brunt of the attack fell on three companies of the 1st Battalion, the King's Own Scottish Borderers, who were holding a 3,000-yard front. The positions ran along ridges roughly shaped like a broad arrow. The whole position had once been part of the Chinese winter defence line. The previous month, it had been stormed and captured during a five-division UN advance, which had marked Commonwealth Division's debut as a self-contained division.

Chinese artillery bombardments and increased enemy activity in the area alerted the UN forces to the forthcoming attack. They responded with an artillery barrage and three airstrikes against the Chinese-held ridges opposite the King's Own Scottish Borderers' line. By noon, the Chinese began firing airburst rounds, clearly indicating that an attack was imminent. These airburst shells were aimed not just at the forward positions, but also battalion headquarters and supply points immediately behind the front line in an attempt to disrupt the support for the men on the front line. At about 1600, the heavy barrage began. In just one hour, the Chinese fired six thousand rounds into the King's Own Scottish Borderers' trenches, destroying the barded wire and severing the field-telephone wire. This barrage continued even when the Chinese infantry reached the battalion's lines and engaged the Borderers.

In the failing light, the Chinese gained a stronghold on the hinge of the Borderers' line. Hundreds of Chinese fell upon two platoons of C Company at this point, who held them off in hand-to-hand fighting. The Borderers were not helped by the poor range settings of their own 2-inch mortars. Time and again, their positions were illuminated by their very own parachute flares.

At 0200 on 5 November, these platoons were ordered to withdraw. The survivors fought their way out through the encircling Chinese, bringing wounded comrades with them. Armed jeeps forayed into the Chinese lines looking for any survivors who may have been left behind, and it is thought that few wounded fell into Chinese hands.

When the Borderers withdrew from the central hinge position, they left nothing between the Chinese and the battalion's heavy mortars. The mortar platoon continued to fire as ordered, its six 3-inch mortars firing about five thousand rounds in four hours before retiring as the Chinese closed in.

On the right of the line, D Company were forced to abandon Hill 317, while on the knoll in between, the enemy appeared 'from what must have been dugouts and bunkers dug the night before under our very noses'. The two platoons there had twelve Bren guns between them, but early in the battle they could not be raised on the radio and their positions were considered lost.

United Hill, the position at the left of the line, had been held by B Company. But Chinese rocket launchers and self-propelled guns had knocked out all the observation posts and machine-gun positions. The platoon holding Hill 217 was soon overrun and the survivors crawled back to the Battle Patrol, which remained in its central position in reserve. The loss of Hill 217 turned the flank of the positions on United Hill, so the company pulled back to the reverse slope to positions previously prepared on the orders of Major Harrison, the commanding officer of B Company.

From there, men with Bren guns and grenades wrought a terrible toll on the Chinese as they charged over the crest, silhouetted against the light of the parachute flares beyond, before they were finally withdrawn. It was then that Private William Speakman came into his own.

Speakman was not even a Borderer, or even Scottish. Born in Altrincham near Manchester in 1927, Speakman joined the Army Cadet Corps as a drummer boy at the age of fifteen. At the age of eighteen, in 1945, 'Big Bill' – who already topped six foot seven – joined the Army. Although he was from Cheshire, he had a dark, Scottish look and it was thought appropriate that he join Highland regiment, so he enlisted in the Black Watch (Royal Highlanders). Bill Speakman's personality matched his frame, but he had a reputation as a gentle giant. He was slow to rouse and disliked telling other people what to do. So he served as a private in Trieste, Hong Kong and postwar Germany. It was there that he volunteered for action in Korea.

Attached to the King's Own Scottish Borderers, he was picked as a runner by Major Harrison. Gallant officer though

Major Harrison was, he was no mountaineer, and part of Speakman's job was to help his commanding officer negotiate obstacles on the steep hillside. But that night everyone was thrown into the action. Major Harris ordered Speakman to cover the crest of the hill, although he already had a painful wound in the leg. This riled him and he vented his anger on the oncoming Chinese.

At the height of the battle, Speakman, with the aid of six men from his battalion, organised an attack that held the Chinese attack off. Testimonies from witnesses said Private Speakman was fighting on the ridge top, tossing grenades at the Chinese, as they climbed towards the King's Own Scottish Borderers' positions. When he ran out of grenades, he ran down to the ration pit, grabbed a new supply and returned to the ridgeline to resume his assault on the Chinese. When a machine-gun post was knocked out and in danger of being overrun by the Chinese, Speakman organised his men to defend the weapon and prevent the Chinese turning it on the Borderers. His action gave his company time to withdraw to safety. Much has been made of the fact that, when he ran out of ammunition, Speakman continued to bombard the enemy position with stones, tin cans and, in particular, beer bottles – Speakman's Victoria Cross became known as the 'Beer-Bottle VC'. But his own account of the action on United Hill was more prosaic.

'We were out reinforcing the wire and had a funny feeling that something was going to happen,' he recalled. 'Two or three hours later, all hell broke loose. There were thousands of Chinese – they must have concealed themselves like rabbits in the ground. There were very skilful at it. It was getting dark and we could only just pick them out. They came at us in a rush all along the front. There was a lot of hand-to-hand.'

The Chinese came in three waves. The first two were cannon fodder who flattened the wire – 'then the third were the really tough ones, and you have to mix it with them. There were so many of them, you just had to get on with it.'

He recalled that there were so many Chinese around him that there was no time even to pull the bolt back on his rifle, 'so you had to fight with the butt of your rifle and the bayonet'. When they ran out of ammunition, they started throwing rocks and stones and anything else they could lay their hands on – but no beer bottles.

'Where would you get bottles of beer from?' he said. 'It's true we did run out of ammunition and we were in darkness, so you pick up what you can get your hands on – fallen weapons or stones … Whoever started the story, it seems to have caught on.'

According to witnesses, Speakman led up to fifteen countercharges.

'We had to get our wounded,' he explained. 'We couldn't just give in – we'd fought so long we couldn't just give up that bloody hill. You were fighting for your life and it's your job to hold the line. If you give in they'll attack the other units from the rear.'

Orders came to withdraw, but Speakman went forward to clear the hill and get the wounded to safety. Eventually, the fighting subsided and the Borderers collected the survivors. Speakman himself wounded by shrapnel in the shoulder and the leg.

'To be honest, you get hit and you don't realise it,' he recalled fifty years later. 'You're a bit busy, and someone says, "Bill, you've been hit in the back."'

He was ordered off the hill to get his wounds dressed, but the medical orderly attending him got caught in a burst of fire.

'I said, "Stuff it" and went forward again.'

Later, Bill Speakman flaked out unconscious and ended up in hospital in Japan. Thanks to the courage of Private Speakman and his comrades, the Chinese attack failed, costing the enemy more than a thousand dead. The Borderers lost seven killed, 87 wounded and 44 missing.

The citation to Private Speakman's Victoria Cross read:

From 0400 hours, 4 November 1951, the defensive positions held by 1st Battalion, The King's Own Scottish Borderers were continuously subjected to heavy and accurate enemy shell and mortar fire. At 1545 hours, this fire became intense and continued thus for the next two hours, considerably damaging the defences and wounding a number of men.

At 1645 hours, the enemy in their hundreds advanced in wave upon wave against the King's Own Scottish Borderers' positions, and by 1745 hours fierce hand-to-hand fighting was taking place on every position.

Private Speakman, a member of 'B' Company, Headquarters, learning that the section holding the left shoulder of the company's position had been seriously depleted by casualties, had had its NCOs wounded and was being over-run, decided on his own initiative to drive the enemy off the position and keep them off it. To effect this he collected quickly a large pile of grenades and a party of six men. Then, displaying complete disregard for his own personal safety, he led his party in a series of grenade charges against the enemy; and continued doing so as each successive wave of enemy reached the crest of the hill. The force and determination of his charges broke up each successive enemy onslaught and resulted in an ever-mounting pile of enemy dead.

Having led some ten charges, through withering enemy machine-gun and mortar fire, Private Speakman was eventually severely wounded in the leg. Undaunted by his wounds, he continued to lead charge after charge against the enemy, and it was only after a direct order from his superior officer that he agreed to pause for a first field dressing to be applied to his wounds. Having had his wounds bandaged, Private Speakman immediately rejoined his comrades and led them again and again forward in a series of grenade charges, up to the time of the withdrawal of his company at 2100 hours.

At the critical moment of the withdrawal, amidst an inferno of enemy machine-gun and mortar fire, as well as grenades, Private Speakman led a final charge to clear the crest of the hill and hold it, whilst the remainder of his company withdrew. Encouraging his gallant but by now sadly depleted party, he assailed the enemy with showers of grenades and kept them at bay sufficiently long for his company to effect its withdrawal.

Under the stress and strain of this battle, Private Speakman's outstanding powers of leadership were revealed, and he so dominated the situation that he inspired his comrades to stand firm and fight the enemy to a standstill.

His great gallantry and utter contempt for his own personal safety were an inspiration to all his comrades. He was, by his heroic actions, personally responsible for causing enormous losses to the enemy, assisting his company to maintain their position for some four hours and saving the lives of many of his comrades when they were forced to withdraw from their position.

Private Speakman's heroism under intense fire throughout the operation and when painfully wounded was beyond praise and is deserving of supreme recognition.

After this battle, the Borderers were withdrawn and moved to another sector. They left Korea in August 1952. Speakman was eventually promoted to sergeant.

Although Speakman's VC was awarded by King George VI, it was the first Victoria Cross to be presented by Queen Elizabeth II. He was also given a civic reception in Altrincham. Posted to Singapore, he married and had six children. He later served in Malaya with the SAS, Boreo and Radfan in the Yemen, then part of the British Protectorate of Dhala. In 1966, he retired from the army and returned to England. But times were tough. After 25 years in the service, he found it difficult to settle into civilian life. Work was hard to find. He sold his medals for £1,500 to pay for repairs to his house. He served onboard a passenger line plying between Southampton and Cape Town. After remarrying in 1972, he emigrated to South Africa, where he worked as a security officer in Durban.

In 1982, his medals were sold on for £20,000. They are now in the National War Museum of Scotland in Edinburgh Castle.

Speakman became a Chelsea Pensioner on 1 November 1993 and was among the Pensioners who marched across the Royal Albert Hall arena at the Festival of Remembrance ceremony on 13 November 1993. The following year he returned to South Africa, though he visited London again to take part in the Queen's Golden Jubilee Parade on 4 June 2002.

PART II
MALAYA

In the 1960s, Britain was trying to divest itself of its colonies in the Far East. From 1948 to 1960 it had fought off communist insurgency during the Malayan Emergency. Now it sought to unite Sarawak, its former colony on Borneo, with those on the Malay peninsula to form the independent state of Malaysia, which received wide international recognition in September 1963. However, President Sukarno of Indonesia saw that the new country was a thinly disguised attempt to continue colonial rule and feared it may try to destabilise his own country.

In response, he began to send raids into Malaysia. These grew in size until, in 1965, the British started making retaliatory attacks across the border. The matter was resolved when a coup d'état brought General Suharto to power. He formally ended hostilities on 11 August 1966. The campaign yielded one VC. It was won by a Gurkha.

CHAPTER FOUR

FROM DESERTER
TO VC

LANCE CORPORAL RAMBAHADUR LIMBU
21 November 1965, 2nd/10th Gurkha Rifles

Rambahadur Limbu was born in 1939 in the village of
Chyangthapu in eastern Nepal. While he was a child, his family
died off one by one, leaving only three brothers.

'We were not sure whether we were going to live, either,' he
recalled in later life. 'There was no reason to believe that we
would be spared, but Death had indeed decided to spare the lives
of these three young brothers of the family. This I was to know
after many years while I was under the shower of bullets, but not
a single bullet had my name written on it.'

His father had served with the British Army in World War
Two and had lived long enough to return to Nepal full of proud
memories. He would tell his war stories about how he and his

comrade had fought the Japanese with their kukris, while showing off his scars. Limbu enjoyed his father's stories and they would later encourage him to became a soldier. However, when Limbu was eight, his father died.

Limbu was expected to work in the fields, but he did not take to farming. He was restless and, when he was fifteen, decided to leave the village to join the army. He knew that his older brother would never give him permission to leave, so, without telling anyone, he and two other boys who wanted to be soldiers crept out of the village one day at dawn. With a small amount of money and some old clothes, they headed for a place called Pashpati on the Indian border, where they heard that the British Army recruited. The journey took them over six days.

He joined up as a boy soldier and had a regulation haircut. The recruits had heard that there was fighting going on in a place they had never heard of named Malaya, which was beyond the sea – a thing they had never seen. Yet they were eager to go. Soon, though, Limbu realised that they were only at the beginning of their training and it would be a long time before he got to see Malaya. Then he began to get lonely and homesick.

He and one of his friends decided to return to their village. They changed into civilian clothes and crept out of the depot one night. But they were penniless and would have starved if a lower-caste 'Damai' family had not taken pity on them. The two boys slept in their stable, but refused food that had been cooked for them. It was not the tradition to accept food from someone of a lower caste. Realising the problem, the family gave them some uncooked rice and vegetables, cooking utensils and a fire, so they could cook their own food.

'I have often asked myself the question: why could I not eat the food cooked by the Damai family but why could I eat the food offered by them but cooked by me?' he later mused. 'After all, it was their food I ate! I am not in a position to comment, criticise or contradict the customs and traditions made by my ancestors, but sometimes I feel that we must get rid of some of the inconvenient and painful customs.'

Although his brother was angry with him, he took Limbu back into the house. Limbu found it hard to settle back into the ways of a farmer and regularly cursed himself for deserting the army. But he feared going back in case he was arrested and jailed as a deserter.

At seventeen, he got his brother's permission to leave the village again. He went to Darjeeling, then on to Sikkim, where he worked felling trees and fell in love. He did not have enough money to marry the girl, but she told him that this did not matter, since her family was rich enough to support both of them. Offended by the suggestion, Limbu returned to his village. There, he and his older brother decided that he should return to Sikkim, marry the girl and bring her back to the village with him.

By then, Limbu's younger brother was old enough to join the army. He had already spoken to the *gallawal* – the local recruiter – from the Jalapahar Recruiting Depot, who had been charge with recruiting 22 men from that district of Nepal. He had 21. Limbu decided to travel back to India with the recruiting party, but with no intention of joining up again. He just wanted the company on the trip. The *gallawal* however, took it for granted that he was one of the recruits. On the way, they got drunk on *rakshi* – the local rice wine – and, in his cups, Limbu said, 'Yes, I'll join the army.'

At the depot, Limbu was terrified that he would be recognised, but he had changed a lot in two years. At fifteen, he had been four foot ten. Now he was five foot three without his shoes. Passed fit, he had the number '10' painted on his chest. This meant he was going in to the 10th Princess Mary's Own Gurkha Rifles.

In the morning, the recruits were drilled. In the afternoon, they were taught to read English. Around town, he saw soldiers on leave from Malaya. They had plenty of money and were surrounded by girls. For the first time, Limbu found that it felt good to be a soldier.

In Calcutta, Limbu and his fellow recruits boarded a troop ship. Limbu was amazed to see the limitless ocean and the flying fishes. Although they were not allowed ashore at Rangoon, they could see the golden pagodas from the ship. Then they sailed on to Penang, where they took a train to their training camp at Sungei Patani.

The training was gruelling and Limbu found it difficult to cope with the heat and the blazing sun. But with plenty of exercise and double rations, including milk and fresh fruit, he began to feel strong and tough.

After ten months, Limbu was selected for the 2nd Battalion of the 10th Gurkha Rifles and in late October 1958 he was sent to join his battalion at Majadee Barracks in Johore Bahru, Malaya. The Malay Emergency was almost over and Limbu had few opportunities to go on jungle operations. They laid a few ambushes, but never got to see the enemy alive, though he saw a few dead ones who had been killed by the 1st Battalion in the district of Pengarang.

After two years with the battalion, Limbu went home on leave. The girl in Sikkim was forgotten about and he married a girl from his own village named Tikamaya in March 1961. He had to return to his battalion soon after. Too junior to be entitled to married quarters, he had to leave her behind. A few months later, when he was in Blakang Mati Singapore, he got a letter saying his first son, Bhakte, had been born.

Promoted to lance-corporal, he was on his second leave in early 1964 when the troubles in Borneo and Sarawak started. When he returned from leave, he left his wife and child with the unit at Blakang Mati, while he moved on to Borneo to join the battalion. In November 1964, he found himself in the jungles of Sarawak, hunting Indonesian guerrillas. They had several contacts with the enemy, but suffered few casualties.

Limbu was a superstitious man and believed in premonitions. In November 1965 he was on jungle operations in Sarawak, where they rarely slept. On 20 November, he had a strange feeling that his unit would be involved in heavy fighting and that he would be responsible for its success or failure. That night he dozed off and had a vivid dream. His section were marching forward, rifles in hand, when their way was blocked by a glowing red arc of fire. It looked like a big red sun on the ground. All the other men stepped back, but Limbu stayed where he was, looking into the fire. He looked back at his men and beckoned them to follow him, but they were afraid and took another step back. Then, without any sense of fear, Limbu marched on into the fire, expecting to be burned. But, once he was inside it, he felt nothing but a strange sense of bliss. Then he woke up.

In the morning, Limbu was drinking his tea and cooking his breakfast alongside Rifleman Bijuliparsad Rai and Rifleman Kharkabahadur Limbu, who were unusually silent that morning. Bijuliparsad was a great eater and Rambahadur Limbu usually gave him some of his own rations to prevent him going hungry. But that morning Bijuliparsad ate little and did not finish his own rations, let alone have any of Limbu's. Limbu asked him want the matter was. He said he did not feel well and he clearly looked sad and uncomfortable.

That afternoon, Limbu and fifteen other Gurkhas came across a strong enemy force in the border area. They outnumbered Limbu's unit by two to one and were dug in on the top of a hill with a sheer drop either side. The only approach was along a knife-edge ridge, wide enough for only three men to advance abreast. Worse, it was guarded by a man in a slit trench with a machine gun.

Limbu led the attack, inching himself forward. He was still 10 yards from the sentry when he was spotted and the machine gun opened up. Bijuliparsad, to his right, was hit and Limbu saw blood on his face.

'As soon as I saw his blood, my own blood began to boil,' Limbu said. 'I swore that the enemy would pay for this with their blood. Blood for blood and nothing but blood could settle this account. For a few moments I could think of nothing else.'

Rushing forward, Limbu reached the trench and killed the

sentry. The enemy were now fully alerted and rained down heavy automatic fire on the trench. But Limbu was determined to lead from the front. With complete disregard for his own safety, he left the comparative safety of the trench and led his men forward to a better firing position some yards ahead. He tried to signal back to his platoon commander the position of the enemy force, but his shouts could not be heard over the explosions of grenades and his hand signals could not be seen for the smoke.

Looking back, he saw both Bijuliparsad and Kharkabahadur lying wounded.

'I had to take them away into safety, otherwise they were going to be an easy target for the enemy,' he said. 'I was more than ready to gamble my one life for those of these, my young riflemen.'

The enemy had already seen Limbu and directed their fire at him. Bullets whizzed over his head.

'Fortunately bullets always tend to travel higher if not correctly aimed and it is not always easy to aim correctly in action at a moving human target,' he said. 'A man with small stature like me has, therefore, some advantage.'

Using what little cover there was, he crawled forward in full view of at least two enemy machine-gun posts which, at this stage of the battle, could not be suppressed by the fire of his own platoon. For a full three minutes, he edged his way forward until he was within touching distance of his friends, but was then driven back by the intensity of fire. After a brief rest, he tried to edge his way forward again. Again he was driven back. Then he realised that speed rather that stealth was his best protection. He raced forward and flung himself down next to one of his wounded comrades. Calling for support from two of the platoon's machine-guns that had moved up on the right, he picked up the wounded man and carried him to safety.

When he returned to the top of the hill, Limbu found that the enemy machine-gunners had increased the weight of fire to prevent any further attempt at rescue. He rushed forward again, making short stops in any meagre shelter that presented itself along the way. At one point he was pinned down for several minutes by the intensity of automatic fire hitting the ground all around him. Eventually, he reached the wounded man, picked him up and raced back through a hail of bullets, this time unable to seek cover.

This daring rescue took over twenty minutes. During the entire action he had been in full sight of the enemy and under almost continuous automatic fire. That he survived the hundreds, if not thousands, of bullets fired at him without a scratch is nothing short of miraculous. But he was not finished yet.

'It took some time but I was able to take my two riflemen into safety and I immediately joined my friends, who were exchanging fire with the enemy,' he said.

He recovered the machine gun abandoned by the wounded men and went back in to take his revenge on the enemy.

'Within an hour we killed all of them,' he said. 'At the end of the battle four of them tried to escape, but they could not escape from our bullets.'

In the hour-long battle, much of it fought at point-blank range, at least twenty-four Indonesians died, while the Gurkhas lost three killed, two wounded. Now it was over.

'At last we had time to rest and relax,' he said. 'The most incredible thing of this action was that I had never hoped to live to see another day. Yet I was still alive. It must have been my lucky day.'

But it was not just luck. In Rambahadur Limbu's own account, he says that whatever was achieved that day could not have been done without the brilliant planning and leadership of his commanding officer, Lieutenant Colonel P O Myers, and his company commander, Captain C E Maunsell.

When Limbu returned from Sarawak in early 1966, he found that his wife was ill. She had not been well since the birth of their second son five months before. On 2 February 1966, she was admitted to the British Military Hospital in Singapore and died there two days later.

'It was the darkest day of my life,' he said.

When the doctors asked him to sign papers giving his permission to perform a postmortem, he lost control, shouting like a madman in his own language, which few present understood. The following day he signed. His wife was buried with full military honours in Ulu Pandan Cemetery.

Limbu was lost without her. His life felt empty and he could not go about the normal routine of the regiment. He decided to leave the army because it reminded him of her. But, when he requested permission to leave, his superiors would not give him a firm answer one way or the other.

He had a vague recollection of the adjutant taking him to the officers' mess to have his photograph taken. He did not know what it was about.

'There were rumours among my friends that I was going to

get a medal or something because, they said, I did a good job in Borneo,' he said. 'I vaguely thought I would possibly get a "leaf", which I had seen many officers wearing with their ribbons on their chests.'

But, since he had made up his mind to leave the army, this was immaterial. All he wanted to do was to take his two sons back to his village, then set off to who knows where.

'I just wanted to escape from everything,' he said. 'My wife had taken all my happiness and desires with her to the grave.'

In the middle of this mental turmoil came the announcement that he had been awarded the Victoria Cross. He did not know how to react, whether to be happy or sad. Telegrams and letters of congratulations poured in from every quarter. These Limbu faithfully preserved. One came from General Sir Peter Hunt at the Royal Military Academy, Sandhurst. It read:

I am writing to you as your Divisional Commander and Major-General Brigade of Gurkhas at the time of the action in which you won the Victoria Cross, to send you my best congratulations on your award. Your bravery and conduct throughout was what I have come to expect of a Gurkha soldier, and you have brought undying renown to your Regiment and the Brigade of Gurkhas. Well done!

If you come to the United Kingdom to get your VC from Her Majesty the Queen, I hope you will be able to come to Sandhurst, where the cadets of the British Army will be proud to meet you.

Preparations for his trip to England were begun immediately. According to Limbu, it was the wish of every Gurkha soldier to visit the United Kingdom in the days before they regularly did a tour of duty, or were sent for specialist courses there. Some even hoped to contract TB so that they would be sent to England for medical treatment. Limbu had never dreamed that he would be going to England – let alone going there to see the Queen.

On 31 May 1966, he flew to London with a party of six. He was accompanied by two riflemen, his platoon Sergeant Harkabali Rai, his platoon commander Lieutenant Ranjit Rai, who had visited England before, and his company commander Captain Maunsell, who would help with the language and customs. Limbu's eldest son Bhakte would join them later.

They stayed at Captain Maunsell's parents' house, where Mrs Maunsell provided plenty of chicken and rice so that they could make their own curry in her kitchen. They were also invited to a reunion of the VC and GC Association, where he met other VC and GC winners. Then they paid a flying visit to Scotland – 'the heaven of whisky and tartan' – staying at Edinburgh Castle.

On 12 July 1967, Limbu went to Buckingham Palace, which he found quite overwhelming. The Queen spoke to him – Colonel Wylie was on hand to translate. After the investiture, the Queen said that she wanted to met Bhakte who was waiting, with Gurkha Major Balbahadur in a private room of the palace. Limbu learned later, much to his chagrin, that five-year-old Bhakte was reluctant to meet the Queen. What was more, he had brought some caps with him, which he unrolled,

'I hope he has not brought the gun as well,' said the Queen.

While in London, Limbu also stopped off at the stock exchange, which in those days still had a trading floor. He was immediately recognised. The traders stopped and applauded him for a full three minutes. The chairman of the exchange then came to greet him and the trading floor gave him another standing ovation. Never before had the world's leading financial institution been brought to a halt in this manner.

In 1967 Limbu married again. On a train from India to Nepal he had his baggage stolen and lost his Victoria Cross, along with his other medals. Later, his regiment gave him replicas and, after that, the RAF flew him direct to Kathmandu every time he wanted to go home on leave. He has since visited Britain several times and has concluded, that it is 'a cold place full of warm people'. Since leaving the army he has lived in Punimaya, Nepal.

PART III
VIETNAM

During World War Two, Vietnamese guerrillas fighting the Japanese had been supported by the US. But in 1945 it was the British who took the Japanese surrender in Vietnam. In an attempt to justify reoccupying their own colonies in Asia, the British rearmed the Japanese to hold Vietnam until the French, the former colonial power in Indochina, were able to return.

Soon afterwards, the Indochina War broke out between the Vietnamese guerrillas and the French forces. This ended with a humiliating defeat for the French in May 1954 at Dien Bien Phu. As the Communists had already established a government in Hanoi in the north and French bureaucrats ran the south, a peace conference in Geneva decided that the country should be split for administrative purposes along the seventeenth parallel, separated by a five-mile demilitarised zone, until an election could be called to unite the country.

However, fearing the spread of Communism in Europe and Asia, the US reasoned that, by fair means or foul, the Communists were bound to win any election in a unified Vietnam. So they encouraged the South Vietnamese politician Ngo Dinh Diem to establish the non-communist Republic of Vietnam in the south.

Having already witnessed Communist insurgency in Malaya, Australia also feared its encroachment. So, when Ngo Dinh Diem requested security assistance from the US and its allies, Australia responded with thirty military advisers, dispatched as the Australian Army Training Team Vietnam (AATTV), also known as 'the Team'. Their arrival in South Vietnam during July and August 1962 was the beginning of Australia's involvement in the Vietnam War. In August 1964 the Royal Australian Air Force (RAAF) also sent a flight of Caribou transports to the port town of Vung Tau.

By early 1965, when it had become clear that South Vietnam could not stave off the Communist insurgents, known as the Vietcong, and their North Vietnamese comrades for more than a few months, the US began a major escalation of the war. By the end of the year it had committed 200,000 troops to the conflict, turning Vietnam into a 'proxy war' between the US and Vietnam's principal supporter, the Soviet Union. As part of the build-up, the US government requested further support from friendly countries in the region, including Australia. While the British refused to participate, the Australian government dispatched the 1st Battalion of the Royal Australian Regiment

(1RAR) in June 1965 to serve alongside the US 173rd Airborne Brigade in Bien Hoa province.

The following year the Australian government felt that Australia's involvement in the conflict should be both strong and identifiable. In March 1966 the government announced the dispatch of a taskforce to replace 1RAR, consisting of two battalions and support services, including an RAAF squadron of Iroquois helicopters. These were to be based at Nui Dat, Phuoc Tuy province. Unlike 1RAR, the taskforce was assigned its own area of operations and included conscripts who had been called up under the National Service Scheme, introduced in 1964. All nine RAR battalions served in the taskforce at one time or another, before it was withdrawn in 1971.

At the height of Australian involvement it numbered some 8,500 troops. A third RAAF squadron of Canberra jet bombers was also committed in 1967 and destroyers of the Royal Australian Navy joined US patrols off the North Vietnamese coast. The Royal Australian Navy also contributed a mine-clearance diving team and a helicopter detachment that operated with the US Army from October 1967.

In August 1966 a company of 6RAR was engaged in one of Australia's heaviest actions of the war, near Long Tan. After three hours of fierce fighting, during which it seemed the Australian forces would be overrun by the enemy's greater numbers, the Vietcong withdrew, leaving behind 245 dead and carrying away many more casualties. Eighteen Australians were killed and 24 wounded. The battle eliminated Communist dominance over the province.

1968 began with a major offensive by the Vietcong and North Vietnamese Army, launched during the Vietnamese lunar-new-year holiday period, known as 'Tet'. Not only the timing but the scale of the offensive came as a complete surprise, taking in cities, towns and military installations in South Vietnam. While the 'Tet Offensive' ultimately ended in military defeat for the Communists, it was a propaganda victory. US military planners began to question whether a decisive victory could ever be achieved and the offensive turned the US public against to the war. For Australian troops, the effects of the offensive were felt around their base at Nui Dat, where a Vietcong attack on targets around Baria, the provincial capital, was repulsed with few casualties.

By 1969 antiwar protests were gathering momentum in Australia. Opposition to conscription mounted as more people came to believe the war could not be won. A 'Don't Register' campaign to dissuade young men from signing up for conscription gained increasing support and some of the protests grew violent. The US government began to implement a policy of 'Vietnamisation', the term coined for a gradual withdrawal of US forces that would leave the conduct of the war in the hands of the South Vietnamese. With the start of phased withdrawals, the emphasis of the activities of the Australians in Phuoc Tuy province shifted to the provision of training to the South Vietnamese Regional and Popular Forces, or Ruff-Puffs, and the Montagnard hill tribes.

At the end of April 1970, US and South Vietnamese troops were ordered to cross the border into Cambodia. While the invasion succeeded in capturing large quantities of North Vietnamese arms, destroying bunkers and sanctuaries and killing enemy soldiers, it ultimately proved disastrous. By bringing combat into Cambodia, the invasion drove many people to join the underground opposition, the Khmer Rouge, irreparably weakening the Cambodian government. When the Khmer Rouge came to power in April 1975, it imposed a cruel and repressive regime that killed several million Cambodians. The extension of the war into a formally neutral sovereign state, inflamed antiwar sentiment in the United States and provided the impetus for further antiwar demonstrations in Australia. In the repeated Moratoriums of 1970, more than 200,000 people gathered to protest against the war, in cities and towns throughout the country.

By late 1970 Australia had also begun to wind down its military effort in Vietnam. The 8th Battalion departed in November but, to make up for the decrease in troop numbers, the Team's strength was increased and its efforts, like those of the taskforce, became concentrated in Phuoc Tuy province. The withdrawal of troops and all air units continued throughout 1971 – the last battalion left Nui Dat on 7 November, while a handful of advisers belonging to the Team remained in Vietnam into the following year. In December 1972 they became the last Australian troops to come home, with their unit having seen continuous service in South Vietnam for ten and a half years. Australia's participation in the war was formally declared at an end when the Governor-General issued a proclamation on 11 January 1973. The only combat Australian troops remaining in Vietnam were a platoon guarding the Australian embassy in Saigon, which was withdrawn in June 1973.

In early 1975 the Communists launched a major offensive in the north of South Vietnam, resulting in the fall of Saigon on 30 April. In the previous month an RAAF detachment of seven or eight Hercules transports flew humanitarian missions to aid civilian refugees displaced by the fighting and carried out the evacuation of Vietnamese orphans in Operation Babylift, before finally taking out the remaining diplomatic staff on 25 April.

From the time of the arrival of the first members of the Team in 1962, some 50,000 Australians, including ground troops and air force and navy personnel, served in Vietnam; 520 died as a result of the war and almost 2,400 were wounded. The war was the cause of the greatest social and political dissent in Australia since the conscription referendums of World War One. Many draft resisters, conscientious objectors and protesters were fined or jailed, while soldiers who served in Vietnam met a hostile reception on their return home. Despite the antiwar sentiment, four men in particular served with distinction in Vietnam, winning the Victoria Cross.

CHAPTER FIVE

DASHER'S DAY

WARRANT OFFICER KEVIN WHEATLEY
13 November 1965, Australian Army Training Team Vietnam
(Posthumous)

Kevin 'Dasher' Wheatley was born in Sydney on 13 March 1937. Educated at Maroubra Junction technical school, he worked as a milk carter, food steriliser, brick burner and machine operator. He married in 1954 and enlisted in the Australia Army in June 1956. He was posted to the 4th Battalion of the Royal Australian Regiment in September and then to the 3rd Battalion in March the following year. He saw his first active service with the 3rd Battalion in Malaya from 1957 to 1959. In August 1959 he joined the 2nd Battalion and in June 1961 was transferred to the 1st Battalion. He was promoted to lance corporal on 19 January 1959, corporal on 2 February 1959 and sergeant on 1 January 1964.

Short and stocky, with dark features, he was one of the best-known and best-liked of the sergeants in the regiment. He was known as a wild man, and gained a reputation on the football field that earned him the nickname 'Dasher'. Never a spit-and-polish soldier, he was known for his persistent good humour and his practical ability as a rough-and-ready fighting man. Asked by his company commander why he wore the heavy equipment on his belt so loosely, he replied that the constant slapping of the pack on the back of his thighs was the only thing that kept him going.

On 16 March 1965, he joined the Australian Army Training Team in Vietnam as a temporary warrant officer class II. He spent six months with a Vietnamese battalion in Quang Tri province, near the border that separated the American-backed South Vietnam from the Communist North. He had been in Vietnam for only a few weeks when he began to make an impression on the Vietnamese and the American advisers. On 28 May, the battalion he had been seconded to was acting as a blocking force for the Army of the Republic of Vietnam (ARVN) – the South Vietnamese army – who were attacking a Communist battalion trapped in a hamlet. The ARVN assault was supported by heavy fire from .50 calibre machine guns. Stray bullets that overshot their mark were raining down on his command post, forcing Wheatley and the rest of the headquarters staff to take cover in a ditch beside the dirt road. A Vietnamese woman with three small children who found themselves caught up in the action also took cover in the ditch beside the command post. As the machine-gun fire became more intense, one of the children, a three-year-old girl, broke loose from her mother and ran screaming across the road.

Disregarding the heavy fire, Wheatley jumped up from the ditch, ran across the road and scooped up the child in his arms. Shielding her with his body, he dashed back to the ditch and safety.

On 18 August, when South Vietnamese troops ceased advancing during an assault, he took the lead and inspired them to continue charging up a hill. His men routed some fifty Vietcong.

In October 1965, Wheatley was posted to Tra Bong with five other Australian warrant officers to relieve the previous group of advisers. This was an area where North Vietnamese Army troops were infiltrating from Laos via the Ho Chi Minh trail. From a Vietnamese Special Forces outpost deep in the enemy-held Tra Bong valley, in Quang Ngai province, the AATTV and American advisers conducted 'search-and-destroy' operations. The advisers were attached to a Civil Irregular Defence Group (CIDG) of Vietnamese tribal and Montagnard soldiers based in an area so isolated that you could get there only by Caribou aircraft operating from a small nearby jungle airstrip.

Daily patrols were conducted from the base. Each day, the probes were gradually moved further outwards. At 0500 on 13 November 1965, Warrant Officer Wheatley set out on one of these operations with the Vietnamese Special Forces A Team, commanded by Second Lieutenant Quang. The operation had been planned by Hungarian-born Captain Felix Fazekas of the AATTV, who had been in Tra Bong since September. The Vietnamese Special Forces were also accompanied by Warrant Officer R J Swanton of the AATTV and Sergeant Theodore F Sershen of the US Special Forces (USSF).

The two-day operation was to be carried out by one

company, plus a reconnaissance platoon and elements of a weapons platoon. The aim was to search and clear an area suspected of harbouring a force of Vietcong guerrillas. The area was roughly triangular, bordered on the north by the main valley road that ran from west to east – on the west by the Nui Hon Doat mountain and the east by the Chap Toi mountain. The only thing unusual about this operation was that the area to be secured was 10 kilometres (6 miles) from the Special Forces base and the furthest they had ventured so far.

It was monsoon season in Quang Ngai and Fazekas wanted the unit to move out half an hour before first light, at 0530, so that darkness would cloak their movements from enemy eyes. They marched in single file down the dirt road for 2 kilometres (1.25 miles). Then, as first light approached, they moved off the road some 500 metres (547 yards) into the jungle. They followed the contour line at the base of the foothills, staying in the jungle and well away from any inhabited area.

At about 1000, the patrol reached the foot of Nui Hon Doat, the western end of the search area, and stopped for a rest. The company commander, Quang, told Fazekas that he did not intend to stick to the jungle, but rather swing northwards, skirting the base of Nui Hon Doat. Fazekas opposed this change of plan, because that way they risked being spotted, but he was overruled.

Once they had moved off again, the patrol neared the edge of the thinning jungle and were seen by a group of peasants working in a paddy field. This area was sympathetic to the Vietcong and, in all likelihood, these men would alert enemy forces to the presence of the patrol.

A 1300, the patrol reached the starting point of the search and divided into three groups. One would move northwest along the main track to Binh Hoa. The second platoon, led by Quang with Sershen and Fazekas, would take a .30 calibre machine-gun and a 60mm mortar and move from the north into the centre of the search area. The third platoon, with Wheatley and Swanton, would move northeast along the Suoi Tra Voi stream, which ran along the foot of the Chap Toi mountain, which marked the eastern edge of the search area.

The centre group had been advancing for twenty minutes when they were fired on from some huts. Returning fire, they flushed out the enemy, who escaped to the west. They were in the process of destroying the huts when they heard gunfire from the east. It was about 1340. Fazekas got on the radio to Wheatley, who assured him that everything was under control. His CIDG were rounding up Vietcong suspects.

The platoon with Wheatley and Swanton had crossed the track to Binh Hoa, just north of a small bridge over the Suoi Tra Voi stream. They now spread out into an open formation to sweep a paddy field that ran between the stream to their right and dense jungle that rose 100 metres (110 yards) to their left. But, as they advanced into the paddy field, they came under fire from the rear and one CIDG man was wounded. Wheatley was in the process of organising his troops for a counterattack when they came under intense automatic fire from a group of huts to the south of the bridge. The fire was so intense that the CIDG were about to break, but Wheatley rallied them ready to make an assault across the stream towards the main Vietcong concentration. Meanwhile, Swanton picked up the wounded CIDG man to carry him to safety.

It soon became clear that the Vietcong force was more than Wheatley's platoon could handle, so he got on the radio and asked Fazekas for assistance. By then, the centre group had reached the village of Vinh Tuy, a kilometre (0.6 mile) to the north. Fazekas halted his unit and hurried over to Quang. He suggested that they turn south to support Wheatley's group, who were now in contact with the enemy. He also suggested that they halt the northerly group and take them south to support Wheatley. But Quang was reluctant to move and a row broke out between the two men.

It was plain to Fazekas that Wheatley was in trouble. His men were facing a company well dug in alongside the paddy field, while the CIDG were in an exposed position with insufficient force to regain control of the situation. With or without Quang, Fazekas was determined to act. He and Sershen broke from their unit and moved from cover to cover south towards the beleaguered Wheatley. Seeing their advisers go, some of the CIDG began to straggle after them.

By 1420, some forty minutes into the action, the CIDG with Wheatley had broken for the jungle, leaving Wheatley alone to provide covering fire for Swanton, still trying to make it to the safety of the jungle to the north with the wounded man. Wheatley poured heavy fire on the enemy positions and managed to suppress the Vietcong fire from the forward weapons pits. But then he saw Swanton drop the wounded CIDG man. He had been shot in the chest. Ducking the bullets,

Wheatley raced across the paddy field and flung himself down beside Swanton. While continuing to return fire, Wheatley radioed Sershen, telling him that Swanton had been badly wounded and requesting an airstrike on the enemy positions and a medevac chopper to get Swanton and the other wounded man out of there.

Sershen and Fazekas were in the jungle-covered ridge above the paddy field some 200 metres (218 yards) from Wheatley and Swanton when the message came through. Fazekas immediately organised the airstrike and the medevac helicopter. Then Sershen heard Wheatley cry out, 'God, somebody help us, somebody do something.' But there was nothing they could do. They were still 150 metres (164 yards) away.

A few moments later, Sershen and Fazekas, along with some fifteen CIDG members who had now caught up with them, emerged through the edge of the jungle, where sporadic fire continued. Fazekas called forward the mortar and machine gun, but they did not appear. Fazekas's group now came under small-arms fire and took cover. They then engaged the Vietcong on the other side of the bridge. Several fell and the others fled. Fazekas and a handful of the CIDG then charged across the stream and into the village, throwing grenades. The remaining Vietcong ran, leaving their machine gun, rifles and dead behind.

Sershen and the rest of the CIDGs stayed behind in the paddy field to cover Fazekas's rear and killed two Vietcong he saw coming down the track. Then he saw at least fifteen Vietcong moving in through the jungle to the east. He shouted a warning to Fazekas, who did not hear him. Crouching down, Sershen and his men took cover, watching as the Vietcong reached the edge of the paddy field. The leader stopped and his men, who had marched single file though the jungle, now bunched up. Sershen leaped to his feet some 60 metres (65 yards) away and poured two magazines of automatic-rifle fire into the group. Seven or eight of them fell dead. The rest ran.

Meanwhile, Wheatley was dragging Swanton across the paddy field. By this time his CIDG members had run for it and he had no covering fire. A CIDG medic dashed over to give Swanton first aid, while Wheatley returned the enemy fire. After bandaging Swanton, the medic told Wheatley that Swanton was dying and tried to persuade him to leave his wounded comrade and make a run for the jungle, but Wheatley refused. He ditched his radio and continued to pull Swanton across the open paddy field while heavy machine-gun fire fell all around.

By the time they reached the edge of the paddy field, Wheatley was out of ammunition and the Vietcong were in hot pursuit. A CIDG member, Private Dinh Do, ran from the cover of the jungle and helped Wheatley drag Swanton the last few yards.

'My platoon and the other platoon that was with us started to run away when I saw WO Wheatley half dragging, half carrying WO Swanton from the rice paddy to some heavy undergrowth,' he said afterwards. 'I helped him in the last stages and asked him to run with us. He refused to leave his friend and pulled the safety pins from the two grenades he had. I started to run when the VC [Vietcong] were about ten metres [33 feet] away. Then I heard two grenades explode and several bursts of fire.'

This was part of Dinh Do's statement in support of the VC

award as given verbally. Dinh Do was illiterate and the statement had to be certified by a thumbprint.

Wheatley and Swanton were caught and killed by the Vietcong, who in turn came under fire from Sershen and his men. Having cleared the enemy's main position, Fazekas and his men came back across the stream to support Sershen. When the firing stopped, the medevac chopper that had been circling the area landed and picked up two wounded CIDGs. No one knew were Wheatley and Swanton were. Soon after, US fighter bombers made an airstrike on the area around the bridge, to little effect, as the Vietcong were long gone.

Quang told Fazekas that he was taking his men back along the track to Binh Hoa. The two men came into conflict again, since Wheatley and Swanton had not been found. But the battle-weary CIDG had had enough, so at 1620 Fazekas got on the radio to Tra Bong and requested that a company of the Nung rapid-reaction forces to be flown in from Da Nang. They arrived by helicopter at a landing zone a kilometre (0.6 miles) up the track from the battlefield at 1800 with Lieutenant Colonel Charles E Ross, the commanding officer of Special Forces in Da Nang.

Fazekas met the incoming troops and led them to a paddy field. They surrounded the area, establishing defensive positions to guard against ambush. By then it was 2230. There was no point in trying to search for Wheatley and Swanton in the dark. While settling down for the night they ambushed two Vietcong infiltrating across the stream.

At 0615 the following morning the Nung began to search.

Private Dinh Do led Fazekas to the spot where he had last seen Wheatley and Swanton the previous afternoon. It was about 50 metres (55 yards) from the jungle edge. They found the two warrant officers' bodies in a hollow nearby. They had been shot in the head. Their bodies were taken to the US Marine Base at Chu Lai, before being forwarded home to Australia.

Among Wheatley's belongings they found eleven pre-drafted telegrams. They were all addressed to the Civic in Sydney, Wheatley's favourite pub. The first said, 'TEN DAYS TO DASHER DAY.' The second said, 'NINE DAYS TO DASHER DAY' ... And so on. The last one said, 'ROLL OUT THE BARREL, THE KING IS HERE.'

Captain Fazekas was awarded the Military Cross for his courage in trying to relieve Wheatley and Swanton. Later that day, back at Tra Bong Special Forces camp, Fazekas filed an after-action report. It read,

I, 48049 Captain F Fazekas, make the following statement: I was the senior AATTV advisor on the 13th and 14th of November 1965 with the CIDG Coy, which went out for a two-day operation. The patrol started from Tra Bong Special Forces Camp at 130500 and moved in an easterly direction along the main Tra Bong valley road to ES 376874. From these coordinates the patrol moved to ES 377868 and moved along the 100-metre [110-yard] contour line to ES 426863. There the patrol had a short rest. While resting, the patrol commander, 2/Lt Quang, LLDB, talked to me and told me that he would not move along the western creek of Nai Hon Dost to ES 445845 where the company was supposed to stay overnight. He instead said he was going to move his company along the jungle edge on the eastern side of the feature. His reason was that the valley in which the original route was planned was too dangerous for his company. After some discussion I agreed to the change of plan. The company moved off and moved very close to the jungle edge on the eastern side and I and also the other advisors, WO2 Wheatley, WO2 Swanton and Staff Sergeant (SSgt) Sershen, agreed that we had been seen by the local population. At 1145 hours the company arrived at ES 445846 and stopped for lunch.

I went to 2/Lt Quang and asked him what were his intentions. He stated that he would follow the original plan and split his company in three groups and continue with the search and destroy operation. As we all thought that surprise was lost, this seemed to be a reasonable plan. The only trouble was the time factor. It was 1300 hours and did not allow us a full day. The force moved then to ES 447846 and one platoon went NW along the main track leading to Binh Hoa (1) ES 435871 without advisors. Another platoon and elements of the weapons Platoon (one MG and one 60mm mortar) moved north in the centre of the valley with me and SSgt Sershen. The remaining platoon and the Combat Reconnaissance Platoon with Wheatley and WO2 Swanton and one MG moved NE following the Suci Tra Voi river.

My element made contact at ES 432852. We sighted four

VC in huts near the area. The VC returned fire and broke in a westerly direction, abandoning one Ml carbine. The huts were destroyed by my element. This happened at approximately 1330 hrs. At the same time there was firing heard from WO Wheatley's group from the east. Upon contacting him on the radio he stated that the CIDG were rounding up some civilian suspects. We continued to advance to ES 450855 where we stopped to allow the flanking platoons to catch up. When I contacted WO2 Wheatley he stated that they were in contact with the VC at ES 453848 but they could handle it. They had one CIDG [member] slightly wounded at this time. He also stated that the CIDG Platoon commander was not doing anything at all and that he had just stopped. I then spoke to 2/Lt Quang and on my radio he spoke to his platoon commander as his radio did not work. 2/Lt Quang then stated that they had three casualties from AR and MG fire. I contacted Wheatley again and asked him about the situation. He still said that they could handle it. Some more conversation took place between 2/Lt Quang and Platoon Commander and at the same time the firing increased. I spoke to WO Wheatley again and he said that they would require help. I told him we were on our way and to Lt Quang to move his platoon into the fight area. He was very reluctant and only when I said I was going anyway did he agree. I moved with SSgt Sershen immediately back taking point scout. The CIDG then slowly started to move also. About halfway back to the fight area SSgt Sershen shouted to me and said that WO Swanton was hit in the chest and that WO Wheatley requested medevac and immediate airstrike on the SE side of the bridge at ES 453847. I radioed immediately to the Tra Bong requesting the above. This was the last time we were in radio voice contact with WO Wheatley.

I continued toward the fight area where heavy firing was still going on and eventually arrived there with SSgt Sershen and about 15 CIDG. I called the mortar and machine guns forward but they did not arrive.

As we broke into the fight area we were engaged by small arms fire. I went to ground and engaged the enemy in the bridge area along the river bank. I had killed or wounded two or three VC, when they broke and started to flee. With about seven to ten CIDG soldiers, I followed them and broke into the village, where the VC broke contact. I saw two VC dead and I grenaded some hides in the village. As there was still firing going on behind me, I moved back to where SSgt Sershen was in contact with the VC. By the time I got back the firing had stopped and the Medevac aircraft was in the area. I guided the helicopters in and evacuated two CIDG wounded. I also told the pilot to look for an Australian wounded (WO2 Swanton) thinking that WO Wheatley might be setting up another LZ [landing zone] in his position.

At this stage 2/Lt Quang stated that he gave orders to the platoon engaged in the fight originally to move back to Binh Hoa (1). Also that he was moving his own platoon back. I told him I would not move without the two Australians. He said that the platoon would be on the track to Binh Hoa (1) and that we could evacuate the wounded Australians from there. I moved back about 500 metres (547 yards) to ES 449849, then to ES 447853. At this time the requested airstrike bombed the southeast end of the bridge and surrounding area.

At this stage I was sure of it, the CIDG would not fight anymore, so I requested the Nung reaction forces to be brought in at 1620 hours. The reaction forces arrived at 1800 hours. I led the reaction forces to the fight area and placed them in two different ambush positions as at this stage it would have been fruitless to search. It was past 2030 hours and very dark. After this I headed over to LtCol Charles E Ross commanding officer of USSF Det C-1.

At 2230 we had one ambush sprung by two VC trying to cross the river. One CIDG slightly wounded. Enemy casualties unknown.

The next morning at 0615 we commenced the search. We found two CIDG KIA [killed in action] and WO2 Wheatley and WO2 Swanton together in a thicket shot through the head several times from close range. We also picked up several weapons, their maps, watches and packs. At 0715 we evacuated them to Chu Lai. After completing the search and medevac the force moved back to Tra Bong.

From the position of the bodies it would be judged that WO2 Wheatley was dragging and carrying WO2 Swanton from the open area to the thicket and stayed there with him, without a weapon, after the CIDG abandoned them, trying to help him and defend him.

The whole CIDG company, after the reaction force came in, claiming that they had no ammunition and that they were tired, moved back to Binh Hoa (1). They were picked up at the same location at 0730 hours on 14 November 1965 and moved back to Tra Bong with the reaction force. The estimated number of VC was a platoon originally in the fight area, then they were reinforced from the village SE of the bridge probably with the remainder of the company. Total casualties were:

Friendly	Enemy
2 AATTV KIA	4 VC KIA Confirmed
2 CIDG KIA	16 VC KIA Unconfirmed
1 CIDG DOW	
[died of wounds]	
9 CIDG WIA	
[wounded in action]	

This was duly signed by Captain Fazekas and witnessed by Sergeant Sershen. It became the basis of Warrant Officer Wheatley's VC award, the first given to an Australian since 1945. The citation read:

Warrant Officer Wheatley enlisted in the Australian Regular Army in 1956. He served in Malaya with 3rd Battalion, The Royal Australian Regiment from 1957 to

1959 and then with 2nd and 1st Battalions of the Regiment until 1965 when he was posted to the Australian Army Training Team Vietnam. His posting in this area has been distinguished by meritorious and gallant service.

On 13 November 1965 at approximately 1300 hours, a Vietnamese Civil Irregular Defence Group company commenced a search and destroy operation in the Tra Bong valley, 15 kilometres east of Tra Bong Special Forces camp in Quang Ngai Province. Accompanying the force were Captain F Fazekas, senior Australian Advisor, with the centre platoon, and Warrant Officers KA Wheatley and RJ Swanton with the right hand platoon. At about 1340 hours, Warrant Officer Wheatley reported contact with Vietcong elements. The Vietcong resistance increased in strength until finally Warrant Officer Wheatley asked for assistance. Captain Fazekas immediately organised the centre platoon to help and personally led and fought towards the action area. While moving towards this area he received another radio message from Warrant Officer Wheatley to say that Warrant Officer Swanton had been hit in the chest, and requested an airstrike and an aircraft for the evacuation of casualties. At about this time the right platoon broke in the face of heavy Vietcong fire and began to scatter. Although told by the Civil Irregular Defence Group medical assistant that Warrant Officer Swanton was dying, Warrant Officer Wheatley refused to abandon him. He discarded his radio to enable him to half drag, half carry Warrant Officer Swanton, under heavy machine-gun and automatic rifle fire, out of the open rice paddies into the comparative safety of a wooded area, some 200 metres away. He was assisted by a Civil Irregular Defence Group member, Private Dinh Do, who, when the Vietcong were only some ten metres away, urged him to leave his dying comrade. Again he refused, and was seen to pull the pins from two grenades and calmly awaited the Vietcong, holding one grenade in each hand. Shortly afterwards, two grenade explosions were heard, followed by several bursts of small arms fire.

The two bodies were found at first light next morning after the fighting had ceased, with Warrant Officer Wheatley lying beside Warrant Officer Swanton. Both had died of gunshot wounds.

Warrant Officer Wheatley displayed magnificent courage in the face of an overwhelming Vietcong force which was later estimated at more than a company. He had the clear choice of abandoning a wounded comrade and saving himself by escaping through the dense timber or of staying with Warrant Officer Swanton and thereby facing certain death. He deliberately chose the latter course. His acts of heroism, determination and unflinching loyalty in the face of the enemy will always stand as examples of the true meaning of valour.

Wheatley was survived by his wife Edna, a son and three daughters. At the time it was Australian policy to bury war dead overseas, but Wheatley's body was returned to Australia after funds were raised privately. He was buried with full military honours at Pine Grove Memorial Park, Blacktown, New South Wales. A public outcry resulted in a government announcement on 21 January 1966 that the remains of service personnel who died overseas would, in future, be returned to Australia at public expense if their families so wished.

His name is commemorated in the New South Wales Garden of Remembrance at Rookwood War Cemetery. In 1967 a trophy for an annual rugby football competition between the Australian Army, Navy and Air Force was inaugurated in his name. A sports arena at Vung Tau in Vietnam and the Land Warfare Centre Canungra Soldiers Club were named after him. His citation and photograph are displayed in the Hall of Heroes, John F Kennedy Center for Military Assistance at Fort Bragg, North Carolina, USA. The United States also awarded him the Silver Star. He was made a Knight of the National Order of the Republic of Vietnam, the country's highest award, and received the Military Merit Medal and the Cross of Gallantry with Palm. In 1993 Wheatley's VC and other medals were presented to the Australian War Memorial, Canberra, where they are now on display.

CHAPTER SIX

THE VC BREED

MAJOR PETER BADCOE

23 February, 7 March and 7 April 1967, Australian Army Training Team
Vietnam (Posthumous)

Major Peter John Badcoe was not a typical Aussie. Short with
a round face, high forehead and heavy glasses, he looked like
someone who would be more at home behind a desk than
on a battlefield. He did not drink or smoke. Nor did he
mix comfortably with his comrades. He was really at ease
only when talking about the exploits of military heroes from
the past.

Born in Adelaide, South Australia, on 11 January 1934, he had
always wanted to join the army, but his father was against it. They
agreed that, if he did a year working and then still wanted to go
to the army, his father would support him. While still at school,

Badcoe played hockey for South Australia and played a fife in the school band. Then he joined the South Australian civil service and bought his first car, a little red MG.

Early in 1952 he served in the 16th National Service Battalion for seven weeks, then on 12 July entered the Officer Cadet School, Portsea, Victoria, graduating as a second lieutenant in the Australian Staff Corps on 13 December 1952.

Early postings included the 14th National Service Training Battalion and 1st Field Regiment, Royal Australian Artillery, though his real passion was the infantry. On field manoeuvres in Australia, Badcoe was known for his energy and aggression. Although an artillery officer, he preferred to lead infantry-style raids on enemy gun positions than use the textbook response of a counterbarrage.

From late 1958 until 1961, he served in the Directorate of Military Operations and Plans at Army Headquarters as a general staff officer grade III. He returned to regimental duties with the 4th Field Regiment on 6 February 1961. In June that year he was posted to the 103rd Field Battery and served a tour of duty in Malaya as a battery captain station at Camp Terendak near Malacca. At the time the American advisers in Vietnam invited the Australians to send observers and in late 1962 Badcoe visited Vietnam for the first time.

While there, he took every opportunity to put himself in the way of combat. Visiting Quang Ngai province south of Da Nang, he was allocated to a battalion for five days. During that short period, the unit undertook three separate operations, all of which resulted in contact with the enemy and one in a pitched battle. During a brief three-hour rest period Badcoe organised a helicopter to take him to a remote spot in the highlands west of Quang Ngai where a Montagnard unit were fighting.

When he eventually returned to Saigon, Badcoe was told that his plane had engine problems and his return to Malaya would have to be postponed for two days. Instead of immersing himself in the fleshpots of the city, he discovered that the 7th ARVN (Army of the Republic of Vietnam) Division were mounting an operation in the Mekong Delta and arranged with the US Military Assistance Advisory Group to be flown south to join it. Within hours, Badcoe was jumping from a helicopter with an ARVN reconnaissance group into a metre of water. The operation extended through the night and, in the morning, they were picked up by boats.

Australian headquarters noted at Badcoe got more than the usual share of operational activity out of his designated role as an 'observer'. Badcoe's own report on the visit read, 'I consider this tour to be of considerable value to all officers of the ARA [Australian Regular Army], in seeing our potential enemy in action and in getting the "feel" of a guerrilla war in a hostile population.'

Badcoe was particularly impressed with one of the American advisers he met, whom he later sought to emulate.

'He spoke Vietnamese,' wrote Badcoe, 'ate Vietnamese rations, displayed considerable courage, and was obviously liked and accepted by the battalion... I consider he is doing an excellent job under highly frustrating circumstances.'

After a third period with the 1st Field Regiment, from

November 1963 to August 1965, Badcoe finally got his way and changed his corps from artillery to infantry. He was promoted to temporary major on 10 August 1965 and posted to the Infantry Centre at Ingleburn, New South Wales. Meanwhile, he and a friend, Captain Ross Buchan, with whom he had served on an artillery battery in Malaya, applied to the Australian Army Training Team Vietnam.

In August 1966, Badcoe realised his ambition to serve in Vietnam when he was posted to the Australian Army Training Team there as a sector operations officer to the Nam Hoa district of Thua Thien province. As an adviser, he was concerned with military operations and training carried out by the Ruff-Puffs (Regional Forces–Popular Forces) in his district, though that was never enough for Badcoe. Within a week of his arrival in Nam Hoa, he accompanied an RF company on a search-and-destroy operation just across the river from the subsector headquarters. They were met with sporadic fire from Vietcong units dug in along a tree line. The company sought to flush them out. They were met with fierce resistance from an enemy bunker whose fire fell among the soldiers of his unit. Far from lending advice – his supposed role – Badcoe tried to silence the bunker single-handed with a rifle and grenade. When that failed the company commander suggested they call in an airstrike. Badcoe said that should not be necessary for five men in a bunker.

He grabbed two jerry cans of petrol from a jeep and ran towards the bunker, whose occupants responded by directing their fire at him. Eventually, he worked his way around to their blind side, poured the petrol over the bunker and ignited it with a phosphor grenade. The resulting inferno was more effective than napalm. The bunker was silenced and the company moved on. It was with such actions that the Badcoe legend was established.

Wearing a red paratrooper's beret, Badcoe was always seen at the head of his men. He seemed convinced of his invincibility – and it rubbed off. His presence was a boost to morale and his courage and audacity made his name a byword for bravery.

In December he was reassigned to the sector headquarters of Thua Thien as operations adviser. Normally, he would have been responsible for planning, liaison and associated staff work, but he took full advantage of the latitude given to advisers to lead forces into action whenever the opportunity arose.

On 23 February 1967 he was acting as an adviser to a regional force company in support of a sector operation in Phu Thu District, in an operation being conducted across the rice paddies of the coastal plains, southeast of the ancient capital of Hué. The Vietcong occupied a number of hamlets there and the RF were to root them out.

Badcoe was with his assistant, Captain James Custar of the US Marine Corps. Six hundred metres to one flank was a PF platoon accompanied by Captain Clement – a subsector adviser from the US Army – and Specialist Sergeant George Thomas, US medical adviser.

It was a hot afternoon with clear visibility as they made their way through the dry paddy fields. In the distance they heard rifle fire. It was too far away to be directed at them and appeared to be coming from the PF platoon to the flank. Custar, who was carrying the radio, passed the message that Clement had been hit. His body lay within 50 metres (55 yards) of an enemy machine-gun position. Further, Thomas had been wounded and was in immediate danger from the enemy. The fire was becoming more intense and they heard the unmistakable rattle of machine-gun fire.

Badcoe sent word to the sector headquarters that he was going to their assistance. Leaving Custar with the RF and with complete disregard for his own safety, he began to jog across the rice paddies towards the sound of fire. He covered more than 600 metres (656 yards) of open ground, which was swept with fire. This grew more intense as he approached the beleaguered men.

The platoon were pinned down. Captain Clement was 150 metres (164 yards) out in front. He had been going to the aid of a wounded PF soldier, when he himself had been mortally wounded. Thomas had gone out after Clement and had been hit and wounded. The rest of the platoon had then withdrawn, leaving the two advisers out in an open area raked by gunfire.

Badcoe quickly assessed the situation. The enemy were dug in along a small rise in the ground. They appeared to be more than a company in strength and the increasing intensity of their fire suggested that they were preparing to make an assault.

Seizing the initiative, Badcoe rallied the platoon and led an attack directly on the enemy position. He raced across the open ground, ducking and dodging to avoid the enemy's automatic fire. Fearlessly, he attacked a machine-gun post that was firing directly at him and killed its crew with his rifle. This inspired the other men. As he urged them on, they charged the enemy trenches and inflicted heavy casualties. Meanwhile, Badcoe carried Clement's body from the battlefield and returned to get Thomas.

'Had it not been for his unhesitant actions and personal courage, I might not have survived the continuous hail of enemy fire,' said Thomas.

Not only had Badcoe avoided a rout, but the platoon went on to defeat a considerably larger force that outnumbered them by a least three to one. For this action, Badcoe was awarded the American Silver Star though, like his VC, it was conferred posthumously.

News of this action had hardly reached headquarters when, on 7 March, the district headquarters at Quang Dien, 13 kilometres north of Hué, came under attack by a Vietcong force with an estimated strength of two battalions. The attack had begun at 0630 and by 0700 the district chief was dead. Now leaderless, the local troops were in a desperate plight and the reaction troops of the RF in Hué were called out. Naturally, Badcoe seized the chance to go with them. But the area was bandit country and they had to drive at speed to avoid ambushes. Riding in the jeep with Badcoe were his assistant and a US lieutenant colonel. Speeding up the road, the jeep veered off the roadway into a ditch, killing the captain. Badcoe abandoned the others and hitched a lift with the Vietnamese company commander.

They found that the village of Quang Dien had already been overrun by the Vietcong. The ARVN headquarters were under attack from three sides. The defenders had already suffered heavy casualties, but were holding out. Badcoe quickly drew up the relieving troop into platoon order, then led them in a dash across an area swept by fire to a position that flanked the enemy. With covering fire from the defenders of the district HQ, he drew his men up into an extended line and charged the main body of the Vietcong. Badcoe commanded the assault from out in front, despite the intense fire. Unprepared for such a ferocious attack, the enemy were forced to withdraw and the besieged headquarters were relieved.

In early April, Badcoe's friend Major Ross Buchan visited him in Hué. They planned to fly to Okinawa for a short leave. Badcoe had written to his wife, telling her of his plans and making no mention of any further operations he was to be involved in before he went. On 7 April Badcoe and Buchan were to travel to Da Nang to await their flight, but, when he dropped into sector headquarters that morning, Badcoe was told that one of the other advisers had reported sick and he was to take over as duty officer. Still hoping to catch his flight, Badcoe saw Buchan off, telling him that he would meet him in Da Nang early the following day.

The job of duty officer entailed taking charge of the operations room, co-ordinating requests for airstrikes or assistance, keeping the situation map up to date and maintaining the operational log. The duty officer was not to leave the operations room without permission and having first secured a replacement. This duty should have involved no danger and should have been a mere inconvenience, a short delay to his leave.

However, as Badcoe went through the incoming signals

traffic, he discovered that all was not going well in a hamlet just eight kilometres from where he was sitting. A small battle was raging at the village of An Thuan, where two companies of Vietcong had established themselves in a fortified position.

The 1st ARVN Division had sent their rapid-reaction force, the elite Hac Bao (Black Panther) Company, with an RF company and a squadron of armoured personnel carriers. But they were in trouble. They had attempted to storm the VC positions, but their first assault had been thrown back with heavy casualties. Their problem was that they had no advisers with them. One had reported sick and, as they were supposed to operate only in pairs, the other did not go. Without advisers, they could not call in an airstrike.

Badcoe knew immediately what he must do. He quickly arranged for a relief duty officer to take over. He summoned his assistant and radio operator, US Army Sergeant Alberto Alvardo, then donned his equipment and checked his rifle and ammunition. The two of them, fully armed, jumped in a jeep and in a matter of minutes were at the battlefield.

Although the Vietcong were outnumbered by the ARVN, they were well dug in with good fields of fire across the open paddy fields. They had no armour but were equipped with mortars, recoilless rifles and machine guns. When Badcoe and Alvardo arrived, the ARVN commander was organising a second assault. This would be led by the South Vietnamese cavalry in their armoured personnel carriers (APCs), followed by the Hac Bao Company, with covering fire from the RF company.

The two advisers clambered into the leading APC for the

assault. Under heavy machine-gun fire, the armoured squadron moved out into the open. They had reached a cemetery some 250 metres (273 yards) from the enemy when intensive mortar and recoilless rifle fire forced then to stop. The cavalry then moved out across the cemetery, finding positions to return fire. Meanwhile, the infantry came up and advanced through them. Badcoe and Alvardo abandoned their APC and advanced with the infantry. As they moved out from the shelter of the cemetery, they were deluged with rifle fire and mortar fragments. The enemy positions appeared impregnable. It was now around 1500.

The infantry had already taken heavy casualties, but when Badcoe reached the front he urged them on. He stood upright in a hail of bullets, trying to rally the troops, who were hugging the ground. But under the intensive fire the infantry slipped back into the cemetery to take cover. The two sides now exchanged fire from under cover. Although the ARVN had armour and a superior number of well-trained troops, there was little they could do but cross a paddy field that offered no cover except for knee-high rice plants. There was a stalemate, while the attackers decided what to do.

An artillery man by training, Badcoe called in the heavy guns. The Hac Bao Company rallied themselves for a third assault. Badcoe took the lead again with Alvardo close behind. He was convinced that, if they could get enough men across the paddy field to fight on equal terms in the village, they would rout the enemy. But things did not go to plan. The artillery barrage on the village halted after a few minutes, failing to keep the enemy distracted while the infantry advanced. No smoke had been provided to cover their movements and there was bad co-ordination with the fire from APCs behind them. And as Badcoe was not the company commander, but merely adviser, he could not take charge. All he could do was to lead by example.

Badcoe set out in front as always, seemingly indestructible. As a fellow adviser said, 'Major Badcoe was always the first into the fray. He never stayed in the centre of his unit to command, but got out in front and led them into battle.'

The Hac Bao followed, to start with at least. Despite Badcoe's fearless leadership, after 150 metres (164 yards), the withering fire proved too much for them. The Hac Bao fell to the ground, trying to hide themselves among the rice plants. Some even attempted to crawl on their bellies back to safety. Realising he was now on his own, Badcoe also threw himself to the ground to take cover, while he figured out what to do next. The one thing he had no intention of doing was falling back. He searched around for the nearest enemy stronghold that was holding up the attack.

Badcoe saw a Vietcong machine-gun position around 100 metres (110 yards) away, lept to his feet and ran towards it. He did not duck or crouch. He intermittently fired at it, then turned to wave his men and the APC on, urging them to follow him. The only person on his heels was Alvardo.

'Major Badcoe didn't waste time trying to tell them to advance again,' said Alvardo. 'He hopped down and started off alone, straight at a battalion of Vietcong. I jumped off the carrier and went after him. Even then he made me proud. While I ran low in the grass he paced out ahead with that silly red Aussie beret bobbing up and down, waving back at the carriers and trying to urge them forward. The mortar bombs were falling all round him like rain, but they might have been Sunday showers for all the notice he was taking.'

Then Badcoe saw a small fold in the ground where he could take cover while he planned his final assault.

'We were getting close to the Vietcong now, real close,' said Alvardo. 'The major just charged ahead, firing at them. A few seconds later we were down in the long grass, and a Vietcong machine gun was only about 27 metres in front, trying to get us.'

Alvardo inched his way up to Badcoe, who was far from done. He pulled the pins on his grenades and leaped to his feet.

'Major Badcoe stood up and started throwing grenades at them,' Alvardo said. But his friend was dangerously exposed. 'So I brought him down with a tackle and they missed.'

Not to be stopped, Badcoe crawled forward a little further and, with bullets whizzing over his head, he leaped up again.

'He hopped up again to throw more grenades,' said Alvardo, 'but this time they were waiting. They got him in the head and he fell. Then I got zapped in the leg. I grabbed the major and started dragging him back towards the carriers. It took me a while to realise he was dead.'

After Alvardo got back to the comparative safety of the cemetery, he called in an airstrike. Two aircraft bombed the VC positions. After another artillery barrage, the ARVN successfully stormed the village.

A memorial service was held in Hué, the largest anyone could recall for an Allied soldier. Colonel Arch Hamblen Jr of the US

Army, deputy senior adviser in I Corps, said, 'He was courageous to an infinite degree – almost fearless, I should think.'

Although, after Wheatley, the Australian government would fly the bodies of servicemen home, Badcoe had elected to be interred in Camp Terendak in Malaysia. He was buried with full military honours, with a bearer party, escort and firing party provided by the 4th Battalion of the Royal Australian Regiment.

Everyone agreed that Badcoe had gone the way he wanted to go, cleanly, with a bullet through his head at the head of his troops. His epitaph read, 'He lived and died a soldier.'

'He was a soldier through and through,' said his widow, Denise.

Back home in Australia, public opinion was turning against the war and there was no memorial service there.

A month before his Victoria Cross was gazetted, US President Lyndon Johnson awarded Badcoe a Silver Star and a First Oak Leaf Cluster. The Oak Leaf Cluster signified a second Silver Star. This was unprecedented. Not only was it being given to a foreigner, the two silver stars were being awarded posthumously on the same day for two different actions. The first was for the rescue of Sergeant Thomas and recovery of Captain Clement's body. The second was for his actions on 7 April. Strangely, news of this award was not covered in the US media. And, of the four Australian winners of the VC during the war in Vietnam, Badcoe is the only one whose picture and citation do not hang in the Hall of Heroes in Fort Bragg, North Carolina.

Major Peter John Badcoe's Royal Australian Infantry Corps' VC was eventually gazetted on 13 October 1967. The citation read:

Major Peter John Badcoe was commissioned as a Second Lieutenant in the Australian Staff Corps in December 1952. He was allotted to the Royal Regiment of Australian Artillery in which he served in a number of Regimental and Staff postings until August 1965. He then transferred to the Royal Australian Infantry Corps and joined the Australian Army Training Team Vietnam in August 1966. He was posted as Sector Operations Officer in Thua Thien Province, South Vietnam.

On 23 February 1967 he was acting as an Adviser to a Regional Force Company in support of a Sector operation in Phu Thu District. He monitored a radio transmission which stated that the Subsector Adviser, a United States Army Officer, had been killed and that his body was within 50 metres of an enemy machine gun position; further, the United States Medical Advisor had been wounded and was in immediate danger from the enemy. Major Badcoe, with complete disregard for his own safety, moved alone across 600 metres of fire-swept ground and reached the wounded Adviser, attended to him and ensured his future safety. He then organised a force of one platoon and led them towards the enemy post. His personal leadership, words of encouragement and actions in the face of hostile enemy fire forced the platoon to successfully assault the enemy position and capture it, where he personally killed the machine gunners directly in front of him. He then picked up the body of the dead officer and ran back to the Command post over open ground still covered by enemy fire.

On 7 March 1967, at approximately 0645 hours, the Sector Reaction Company was deployed to Quang Dien Subsector to counter an attack by the Vietcong on the Headquarters. Major Badcoe left the Command group after their vehicle broke down and a United States Officer was killed; he joined the Company Headquarters and personally led the company in an attack over open terrain to assault and capture a heavily defended enemy position. In the face of certain death and heavy losses his personal courage and leadership turned certain defeat into victory and prevented the enemy from capturing the District Headquarters.

On 7 April 1967, on an operation in Huong Tra District, Major Badcoe was with the 1st ARVN Division Reaction Company and some armoured personnel carriers. During the move forward to an objective the company came under heavy small arms fire and withdrew to a cemetery for cover, this left Major Badcoe and his radio operator about 50 metres in front of the leading elements, under heavy mortar fire. Seeing this withdrawal, Major Badcoe ran back to them, moved amongst them and by encouragement and example got them moving forward again. He then set out in front of the company to lead them on; the company stopped again under heavy fire but Major Badcoe continued on to cover and prepared to throw grenades, when he rose to throw, his radio operator pulled him down as heavy small arms fire was being brought to bear on them; he later got up again to throw a grenade and was hit and killed by a burst of machine gun fire. Soon after, friendly artillery fire was called in and the position was assaulted and captured.

Major Badcoe's conspicuous gallantry and leadership on all these occasions was an inspiration to all, each action, ultimately, was successful, due entirely to his efforts, the final one ending in his death. His valour and leadership were in the highest traditions of the military profession and the Australian Regular Army.

His widow and their three daughters went to Government House for the investiture. For the second time in a few months, the Governor-General, Lord Casey, had to present a posthumous VC to a bereaved family.

'If ever there was a breed of person who wins the Victoria Cross, it was his,' said Denise Badcoe. 'The life in the army was the only work his knew. He volunteered to go to Vietnam. He felt it was his duty. He felt he had a job to do.'

'He was great daddy,' said his seven-year-old daughter Kim. 'I will remember him for ever.'

For his services in Vietnam, Peter Badcoe was also awarded made a Knight of the National Order of the Republic of Vietnam and awarded the Cross of Gallantry with Palm, Gold Star and Silver Star, and the Armed Forces Honour Medal 1st Class. In November 1967 an Australian and New Zealand soldiers' club in Vietnam was officially opened as the Peter Badcoe Club. A training block at the Officer Cadet School, Portsea, was also named Badcoe Hall in his honour. Streets in

Canberra and Sydney are named after him and there is a park named after him in his hometown, Adelaide.

His widow and his three daughters presented his medals to the Australian War Memorial for display in the Hall of Valour.

CHAPTER SEVEN

'POST IT
TO ME'

WARRANT OFFICER RAYENE SIMPSON
6 and 11 May 1969, Australian Army Training Team Vietnam

Like Major Peter Badcoe in our previous account, Ray 'Simmo' Simpson was every inch a professional soldier. He had seen service in World War Two, Korea and Malaya before he turned up in Vietnam. However, during his career, he had had regular run-ins with the army and had been discharged three times at his own request. His most serious difficulties with the military authorities occurred in 1965, when he had been assigned to a desk job in Australia while convalescing after being wounded in the leg. News came through that he had been awarded the Distinguished Conduct Medal (DCM) and he had been invited to Government House in Sydney to receive it.

'Owing to the fact that I was disgruntled with the army

because they wouldn't allow me to return to Vietnam, I refused to attend the investiture,' he told a friend, 'and suggested they post it. Which they did.'

A tough, hard-living, hard-drinking man, Simpson found soldiering in Australia boring. He liked action. He had been one of the first thirty Australian advisers to go to Vietnam in 1962 and spent more time in-country than any member of the Australian Army Training Team Vietnam. Not only did he miss the thrill of combat, but had a personal reason for serving there. He had a Japanese wife named Shoko, whose mother had had a heart attack during her daughter's visit in 1964. Shoko stayed on to tend her elderly mother. Stationed with Commando Reserve in Sydney, he rarely got the opportunity to see his wife. But when he was in Vietnam he could take regular leave in Japan, at government expense.

After he had recovered from his wound, it was found that one leg was shorter than the other and the army declared him unfit for active service. He was furious and caused such a rumpus that there was talk of a court martial. This was prevented only when his commanding officer stepped in. However, the commander of 1 Commando was himself left with a stain on his career and, finding his further advancement blocked, left the army.

Simpson then left in disgust. He took a job as a salesman, but found it hard to adjust to civilian life. So he scraped together the airfare to Saigon and rejoined the Australian Army Training Team. When it was discovered that he was no longer in the army, Simpson said, 'Never mind. Just draw me a weapon and some greens and I'll get cracking.'

He was then asked how he got back to Vietnam without authorisation.

'It's not hard when you've got mates,' he said.

Like Badcoe, as well as being valiant on the battlefield, he was extraordinarily well read, especially in military history. His greatest military hero was Otto Skorzeny, the SS officer who had rescued Mussolini and infiltrated the Germans behind the Allied lines dressed in American uniforms during the Battle of the Bulge. Acquitted at the Nuremberg war-crimes trials when a British officer testified that he had done nothing the Allies would not have tried, he escaped from Darmstadt prison during the denazification trials and fled to Spain.

Simpson was born in Chippendale, New South Wales, on 16 February 1926, and educated at Carlingford and Dumaresque Island public schools in Taree, New South Wales. He joined the second Australian Imperial Force on 15 March 1944 and was sent to the 41st/2nd Infantry Battalion, a unit for soldiers under the age of nineteen. On the morning of 5 August 1944, Simpson had his first taste of action when Skorzeny was part of a detachment sent to reinforce the garrison troops at Cowra, New South Wales, after several hundred Japanese prisoners of war had escaped. One of his duties that day was to man the number one Vickers machine gun. Several hours earlier the crew of number two gun had been killed by the Japanese. He then saw service in New Guinea.

Demobilised in January 1947, Simpson drifted from job to job. During the next four years he was a tram conductor, a builder's labourer, sugar-cane cutter and sailor on ships sailing around Papua New Guinea. He re-enlisted in 1951 to see service in Korea with the 3rd Battalion of the Royal Australian Regiment. He was appointed lance corporal in November 1951, promoted to corporal in January 1953 and made temporary sergeant in January 1954. He took part in the battles over the Imjin River in October 1951 with what one British Army officer said was 'the finest fighting infantry battalion I have ever seen', and was at Hill 317 when Private William Speakman won his VC (see 'The Beer-Bottle VC' above).

It was while he was on leave in Japan in 1952 that he met and married Shoko Sakai, a Japanese citizen, in a Shinto ceremony. This was a typically brave thing to do. World War Two had been over for only seven years and many Australians still harboured a grudge against the Japanese. They stayed together until Simpson's death 27 years later.

He was posted to the 2nd Battalion, RAR, in January 1954. In October they were sent to Malaya and he served with them there for two years, making full sergeant. Simpson was next sent to 1st Special Air Service Company in Perth in November 1957. By now fully conversant with jungle warfare and special operations, he was selected for the first group of advisers of the Australian Army Training Team Vietnam (AATTV) who left by air for Vietnam in July 1962. However, his first tour of duty proved uneventful.

After another year with the Special Air Service unit in Australia, he was restless for action and he volunteered to return for his second tour of duty with the AATTV in Vietnam in July 1964. As a temporary warrant officer class II, Simpson was sent as an adviser to the US and South Vietnamese Special Forces base near the village of Ta Ko on the Laotian border. He helped set up a patrol base to monitor Vietcong and North Vietnamese Army forces infiltrating down the Ho Chi Minh trail over the border there. Although Simpson's role was to advise the local forces, like Badcoe he took the opportunity to go out on patrols through the jungle-covered mountains with them.

On 16 September 1964 he was with a company of South Vietnamese Special Forces when they fell into an ambush. The Vietnamese commander was killed and Simpson was shot in the right leg. Although he found it difficult to stand, he rallied the patrol and formed a perimeter. Together they held off repeated enemy attacks while Simpson radioed for help. By the time the relief force arrived, they were low on ammunition and Simpson was weak from loss of blood. Even then, he had to make sure that the position was secure and his men safe before he was evacuated by helicopter to the 6th Field Hospital at Nha Trang. He convalesced in Tokyo and, on 1 October, his rank of warrant officer class II was confirmed.

After leaving the army again in May 1966, Simpson was back in Vietnam in 1967 for his third tour of duty with the AATTV. When he performed the actions for which he was awarded the Victoria Cross, he was serving in Kontum province, near the Laotian border, as commander of a mobile strike force.

He had been there for about two years when, on 6 May 1969, he was in the jungle west of the Special Forces camp at Ben Het in Kontum province commanding the 232nd Company of Mike Force, which was leading the 3rd Battalion on a search-and-destroy mission through the area where the borders of Vietnam,

Cambodia and Laos meet. This was the homeland of the Montagnard tribesmen, an independent aboriginal people with a historic antipathy towards the Vietnamese, who encroached on their lands. However, it was necessary to get the Montagnards to fight for the South Vietnamese government in Saigon, to prevent Vietcong and North Vietnam Army (NVA) soldiers infiltrating through their homelands.

Once the battalion had cleared the area, they were to set up positions to interdict the enemy as they infiltrated into Vietnam. This was easier said than done. The terrain was rugged. The steep slopes were covered with jungle, interspersed with thickets of bamboo. The ground underfoot was muddy and churned by bomb craters and old weapons pits. The rain was torrential, further limiting visibility. However, the sound of the downpour on the leaves helped cover the noise of the advancing patrol as they slipped and slid and rattled the bamboo.

It was around 1430 and they were barely 2 kilometres from the Cambodian border when the forward platoon approached a jungle clearing. The men were just taking evasive action to get around the open ground when they came under heavy fire. NVA troops had occupied the other side of the clearing in strength. They were well dug-in in camouflaged positions and the platoon was pinned down.

The Montagnards on point returned fire while Simpson mustered the rest of the company and brought them forward. He now led his men into the attack. As they moved from cover to cover, it was plain that the NVA were directing their fire at the big Australian. Suddenly, a second enemy position that had lain concealed opened up with flanking fire. Simpson's assistant,

Warrant Officer M W Gill, who was leading one of the attacking platoons, was hit and fatally wounded. The attack faltered as the Montagnards began to pull back. With no thought for his personal safety, Simpson dashed across the open ground raked with gunfire, grabbed Gill and carried him to safety.

Simpson then returned to the front and, shouting in the Montagnard dialect, interspersed with few choice Aussie phrases, he urged his men to go forward again. But they were in no mood to follow him. Leading by example, he crawled forward to within 10 metres of an NVA bunker and lobbed hand grenades. But, unable to break the enemy's defences, he pulled back and gave the order to withdraw. He and five Montagnards stayed behind to cover the retreat with white smoke from phosphor grenades.

Night was now approaching and Simpson pulled his men back to a helicopter landing zone where the casualties could be evacuated.

'The performance of the company was a damned disgrace both during the contact and subsequently at the LZ, approximately 250 metres north of the scene of the contact,' Simpson later wrote in his after-action report. 'Men refused to manoeuvre or shoot and many in fact moved out of the position to the rear. At the LZ they refused to form a perimeter and laid along the trail.'

With the LZ unsecured, the medevac helicopter was driven off by hostile fire. Gill could not be evacuated and died during the night. At first light, the company pulled back to join the rest of the battalion nearby. Only then could they establish a secure LZ so the dead and wounded could be evacuated.

For the next three days, the battalion remained in position so that they could regroup and be resupplied by air. Then, on 10 May, they moved out again. But they had gone only a short distance before they were attacked. Airstrikes had little effect and, again, the Montagnards refused to attack. Simpson was forced to pull back.

The following morning an artillery barrage was brought down on the enemy positions. Simpson's men then moved forward to find the NVA bunkers empty.

At noon, the commanding officer of the AATTV, Lieutenant Colonel R D F Lloyd, arrived by helicopter to assess the situation. He had heard of Warrant Officer Gill's death and knew things were not going well. He found the battalion cautiously probing their way forward through dense jungle towards a steep hill. The operation was being led by the battalion commander, Captain Green of US Special Forces (USSF). With him were 231st Company, led by Warrant Officer B Walsh and Warrant Officer A M Kelly, two other Australian advisers. Simpson, assisted by Specialist Sergeant Peter Holmberg of the USSF, brought up the rear with the 232nd, accompanied by Lieutenant Colonel Lloyd and his assistant, Captain Peter Rothwell, a staff officer at the Special Forces headquarters in Nha Trang.

As they moved stealthily through the undergrowth, there were signs of enemy activity all around them, including fresh tank tracks. Early in the afternoon, Green arrived at another small clearing. As lead elements made their way through the thinning trees there was a burst of heavy fire and Kelly fell wounded. The Montagnards took cover while Captain Green ran to Kelly's assistance and was killed outright by a second burst of gunfire.

Still conscious, Kelly managed to get off a radio message advising an approach along the left flank before he was hit again. Walsh brought a platoon around to the left, but the Montagnards refused to approach the scene of the firing and Walsh continued alone. Simpson could not persuade his men to move forward, either, so he, Holmberg and Rothwell advanced alone. Then began a three-man war.

Under heavy fire, Simpson crawled forward, putting himself between the wounded Kelly and the enemy. Reaching within a few metres of the NVA positions, he began bombarding them with grenades and rifle fire, while Walsh and Holmberg tried to drag Kelly back out of the line of fire.

'I moved to the wounded while Simpson took another section and moved to the left and front to secure myself and the wounded from enemy fire,' said Holmberg. 'Inspecting Captain Green's body, he was dead. When WO Walsh went out to get Green's rucksack the enemy opened up with heavy machine-gun fire. The whole area was sprayed. WO Simpson's area caught the full burst and the tree he was beside was ripped apart.'

By this time, most the Montagnards had disappeared. Those nearby refused even to make stretchers for the wounded in their haste to get back down the hill. Walsh and Holmberg made one themselves and carried Kelly to safety, leaving Simpson alone to hold off the enemy while the others retreated. Not only did Simpson's solo efforts allow the wounded to be evacuated, but he prevented the North Vietnamese advancing and overwhelming his entire force.

To the rear, deserted by the Montagnards, Rothwell single-handedly cleared a landing zone with his machete, so that Kelly and the other wounded men could be medevacked out. But when the helicopter arrived it was driven off by ground fire. Rothwell then cleared the nearby undergrowth of enemy soldiers using grenades and rifle fire so that the wounded could be moved further back. Then he managed to rally some of the Montagnards to hold the enemy at bay until the rescue party reached the main body of the company.

During the entire action, Lieutenant Colonel Lloyd had been on the radio requesting airstrike, artillery and other assistance – only to be told, repeatedly, that other targets had priority. It was after dark before a second medevac helicopter arrived. It then had to make the dangerous manoeuvre of hovering above with trees with its landing lights on, while the wounded were winched aboard. Fortunately, the enemy, who were nearby, did not interfere.

That night passed uneasily. One company was still detached and the NVA probed the loose perimeter the Montagnards had formed. However, airstrikes discouraged the enemy from attacking in force.

The following morning Lloyd and Rothwell flew out. More helicopters were sent to pick up the rest of the battalion. Lloyd flew on to Nha Trang to see the commander of the 5th Special Forces Group to complain. He threatened to pull out the Australian advisers unless significant improvements were made.

The Montagnards were ill-trained, ill-disciplined and had extremely low morale. Artillery and air support were inadequate. Intelligence about the enemy in the area was sketchy at best, resulting in saddle-up-and-follow-me briefings. Throwing ill-trained, ill-briefed troops against numerically superior and well-trained regulars from the North Vietnamese was a reckless waste of life, he believed.

On 21 August, Simpson was summoned to a special conference in Saigon, hosted by the Australian task force commander, Major General R Hay. Two minutes before the meeting began, General Ray dropped the bombshell: Simpson had been award the VC. The citation read:

On 6 May 1969, Warrant Officer Simpson was serving as Commander of 232nd Mobile Strike Force Company of 5th Special Forces Group on a search and clear operation in Kontum Province, near the Laotian border. When one of his platoon became heavily engaged with the enemy, he led the remainder of his company to its assistance. Disregarding the dangers involved, he placed himself at the front of his troops, thus becoming a focal point of enemy fire, and personally led the assault on the left flank of the enemy platoon. As the company moved forward, an Australian Warrant Officer commanding one of the platoons was seriously wounded and the assault began to falter. Warrant Officer Simpson, at great personal risk and under heavy enemy fire, moved across open ground, reached the wounded Warrant Officer and carried him to a position of safety. He then returned to his company where, with complete disregard for his safety, he crawled forward to within ten metres of the enemy and threw grenades into their positions. As darkness fell, and being unable to break into the enemy position, Warrant Officer Simpson ordered his company to withdraw. He then threw smoke grenades and, carrying a wounded platoon leader, covered the withdrawal of the company together with five indigenous soldiers. His leadership and personal bravery in this action were outstanding.

On 11 May 1969, in the same operation, Warrant Officer Simpson's Battalion Commander was killed and an Australian Warrant Officer and several indigenous soldiers were wounded. In addition, one other Australian Warrant Officer who had been separated from the majority of his troops was contained in the area by enemy fire. Warrant Officer Simpson quickly organised two platoons of indigenous soldiers and several advisers and led them to the position of contact. On reaching the position, the element with Warrant Officer Simpson came under heavy fire and all but a few of the soldiers with him fell back. Disregarding his own safety, he moved forward in the face of accurate enemy machine-gun fire, in order to cover the initial evacuation of the casualties. The wounded were eventually moved out of the line of enemy fire, which all this time was directed at Warrant Officer Simpson at close range. At the risk of almost certain death he made several attempts to move further forward towards his Battalion Commander's body but on each occasion he was stopped by heavy fire. Realising the position was becoming untenable and the priority should be given to extricating other casualties as quickly as possible, Warrant Officer Simpson alone and still under enemy fire covered the withdrawal of the wounded by personally placing himself between the wounded and the enemy. From his position he fought on and by outstanding courage and valour was able to prevent the enemy advance until the wounded were removed from the immediate vicinity. Warrant Officer Simpson's gallant and individual action and his coolness under fire were exceptional and were instrumental in achieving the successful evacuation of the wounded to the helicopter evacuation pad.

Warrant Officer Simpson's repeated acts of personal bravery in this operation were an inspiration to all Vietnamese, United States and Australian soldiers who served with him. His conspicuous gallantry was in the highest tradition of the Australian Army.

This appeared in the *London Gazette* of 26 August 1969 and the supplement of 29 August 1969.

'I almost fell over,' said Simpson, when he heard of his award. 'I don't believe it. It's incredible.'

The United States also awarded him the Silver Star and the Bronze Star for Valour, making him the most highly decorated soldier in the Australian Army.

That night there was a party at the Savoy, the Australian

Warrant Officer and Sergeant's club. A large amount of beer was consumed. And Australia's other two VCs from the Vietnam war were not forgotten: Kevin Wheatley and Peter Badcoe were mentioned in the toasts.

Also on hand was Sergeant Peter Holmberg. Simpson put his arm around Holmberg's shoulders and said, 'He was with me on those actions they gave me the VC for. He's a beauty.'

The following day, Simpson was posted to the Mekong Delta, where he was to join a small group of advisers teaching the villagers local defence.

'Ray's new posting is for a definite reason,' said Lieutenant Colonel Lloyd. 'He had four pretty hectic years here so far. A time out of the regular fighting line will do him good. The posting was decided well before the Victoria Cross award was approved.'

Simpson received his Victoria Cross from the Queen during an investiture held at Government House, Sydney, on 1 May 1970. Three days later he left the army. He loved soldiering, but he knew that he would not be allowed to return to active service in Vietnam. He loathed the frustration of a desk job and he wanted to be with his wife, so he moved to Japan to be with her. In fact, he would not even have bothered to go back to Australia to get his VC if his wife had not insisted. Otherwise, as with the DCM, they could have posted it to him, he told a friend.

Asked how he wanted it presented, he said that he did not care 'as long as they give it to me with the cheese and kisses there right beside me'. The *Daily Telegraph* and *Daily News* translated this curious piece of rhyming slang as, 'You know, the Mrs, I want her to be there. She has been through a lot.'

In 1972 he took up a position as administrative officer at the Australian Embassy, Tokyo. But administrative work did not really suit him.

'My job is fair enough,' Simpson told his niece. 'The pay is quite reasonable and the work is easy, but for me very boring. I was never cut out to be a "desk jockey". The outdoors for this bloke.'

And, when the story of the postwar VC winners was recorded by the Australian authorities, Lieutenant Colonel R L Burnard, who had served with Simpson in Korea, Vietnam and the SAS, said, 'He was the most outstanding soldier among an elite group of men. He is a rough and tough sort of bloke, who knows more about soldiering than anyone I know. He's pretty much a loner, a man who knows what he's doing. He embodies all the characteristics that Australians like to think make up the Australian character.'

Simpson died of cancer in Tokyo on 18 October 1978 at the age of 52 and was buried at the Yokohama War Cemetery, Japan. A Requiem Mass was held at St Ignatius Church, Sophia University, in Tokyo. It was attended by representatives of the Australian Army and Navy and the British Army. The eulogy was given by the Australian ambassador John Menadue, who said, 'He will be remembered by many generations of Australians as one of the bravest of the land; but to those who knew him at close hand two things will always remain in our memories. One was his Australianism, something he displayed with pride and without humility. He was the Aussie in all of us. The other was his utter loyalty to his sovereign and his wife. He served his Queen with an abiding passion, and stood by his love with an abounding love.'

Other memorial services were held at the Returned Servicemen's Club in Paddington and the Duntroon Chapel in Canberra, attended by Warrant Officer Kelly, whose life Simpson had saved.

As Simpson had not died in action, Shoko was not eligible for a war widow's pension. And, although she had naturalised as an Australian, she had not lived there long enough to be eligible for social-security benefits. Eventually, the newspapers and ex-servicemen's organisations forced the Australian government to give her an ex gratia pension, though it was considerably less than was given to war widows. She continued to live in Tokyo, looking after her invalid mother though she was suffering from arthritis and hearing loss. In an effort to help out, the Australian embassy offered her a cleaning job. There was an outcry. This was no way to treat the widow of a VC.

The Australian War Memorial in Canberra, who usually only accepted gifts, offered AU$12,000 for Simpson's medals. In the furore that followed, they were forced to up their offer to AU$15,500, which Shoko reluctantly accepted. His medals and a portrait by Joshua Smith are now on display in the Hall of Valour at the Australian War Memorial and his photograph and citation are hung in the Hall of Heroes, John F Kennedy Center for Military Assistance, Fort Bragg, North Carolina.

Eventually, in May 1981, Shoko was awarded a war widow's pension, when it was adjudged that Simpson's cancer might have been caused by the carcinogenic chemical dioxin found in the defoliant Agent Orange that the Americans had sprayed on the jungle to deny the enemy cover during the Vietnam war.

CHAPTER EIGHT

'SOMEONE HAD TO'

WARRANT OFFICER KEITH PAYNE
24 May 1969, Australian Army Training Team Vietnam

After Warrant Officer Rayene Simpson (see previous account) was withdrawn, the bitter fighting continued around the area of Ben Het. All the battalions of 2nd Mike Force Command were committed. Another action took place in almost exactly the same spot as where Simpson had won his VC. And, for the second time in two weeks, Lieutenant Colonel R D F Lloyd found himself writing a recommendation for a VC.

Like Simpson, Keith Payne was a career soldier, a veteran who had fought in Borneo and Korea. He was a family man, married with five sons. But, with his comrades on the field of battle, he was game for anything. And he was an outdoor type. Before he enlisted in 1951, he had been an apprentice cabinetmaker but could not stand it.

'I didn't like confined spaces,' he said, 'and I didn't like the noise.'

A comparative latecomer to Vietnam, he joined the AATTV (the Australian Army Training Team Vietnam) in January 1969 and was sent to the Australia detachment with the Special Forces at Pleiku. There he was given command of the 212th Company of the 1st Mike Force Battalion (MFB), a sister battalion to the one in which Simpson was serving.

This was a difficult time to be taking over. America was already trying to withdraw from Vietnam. Richard Nixon had won the 1968 presidential election on the promise of 'peace with honour' and, when he became president in 1969, he began a policy of 'Vietnamisation': US troops were gradually to be replaced with freshly trained Vietnamese ones. This did not suit the Montagnards in the Special Forces. They had a long-standing hatred of the Vietnamese and in 1964 had rebelled against the Vietnamese officers who, they claimed, had treated them cruelly and stole their pay. Since then, they had not minded fighting as mercenaries under American and Australian command. But now Vietnamese officers were being drafted in again. The Americans and Aussies were expected to stand aside for inexperienced junior officers who were to take joint command. Despite their protests, the advisers were ordered to fly the South Vietnamese flag at all camps and facilitate indoctrination classes. The Montagnards were also supposed to hand over the bounty they got for captured weapons to the Vietnamese officers, which further exacerbated racial antagonism. Morale was at an all-time low. The disaffected Montagnards were then expected to take over from experienced US units. Meanwhile on the other side, the irregular guerrillas of the Vietcong who had practically been wiped out in the Tet Offensive of January 1968 were being replaced by the highly trained regular soldiers from the North Vietnamese Army.

Within a week of taking command, Payne went into action with his second-in-command and fellow Aussie Kevin Latham. They led the company into the mountainous region south of Kontum. As soon as they landed, gunfire was being directed at the helicopters. Quickly rallying his men, Payne counterattacked and fought his way out of the ambush. The first objective – to make contact with the enemy – had been fulfilled before most to the company had landed. Over the next three days of heavy fighting, Payne won the US Silver Star.

In March 1969, Payne's company were in the jungle near Ben Het Special Forces camp in hot pursuit of the NVA who had overrun a post nearby. Although he did not capture his quarry, he did uncover a huge enemy supply dump.

Throughout April and early May there was increased activity in the tri-border area. Payne led his ill-trained troops on an operation to relieve the besieged border camp of Bu Gia Map. This began with another ambush, when the landing again came under fire and the helicopters were forced to set the troops down in bamboo thickets laced with punji sticks – sharpened wooden stakes often smeared with excrement to infect any nonfatal wound. Repeated airstrikes failed to dislodge the NVA. That took two days of close-quarters fighting.

Crossing a river two days later, Payne was knocked out by a machine-gun bullet that grazed his head. Latham charged forward shooting an M-60 from the hip, suppressing the opposition. Then on 25 April – Anzac Day – Payne's company was halted just 2.5 kilometres from camp. Behind a shrinking perimeter, Payne's men fought off enemy attacks for two weeks. They were running low on ammunition and water until a platoon under Warrant Officer Barry Tolley got through to them. Reinforced, the 212th held on until heavy airstrikes forced the NVA to break off on 12 May.

The strength of the enemy's resistance convinced the commander of the 2nd Mike Force Command that the NVA's build-up had some important objective in its sights. Then everything became clear when the Ben Het itself came under siege. Just 14 kilometres from the Lao border, Ben Het sat astride Route 512. This ran east from the tri-border area on to the Special Forces base at Dac To, then south into Kon Tum and the central highlands. Taking Ben Het would give the enemy command of a major infiltration route to the whole of South Vietnam.

The siege began with the 24th NVA Regiment moving in from the north and the 27th from the east, cutting it off from Dac To. Intelligence also indicated the 66th NVA Regiment had infiltrated over the border from Laos to the west to encircle Ben Het completely, but no one currently knew where they were. It fell to the 1st MFB to find them and hold them until reinforcements could arrive.

The battalion was not in good shape. It had been in action for several weeks and was under-strength due to numerous casualties. Its commander was away on leave and command was taken by the executive officer, Lieutenant D James Jr. Warrant Officer Barry Tolley took command of the 211th Company. Payne was in command of the 212th, and the 213th was under Sergeant 'Monty' Montez of the US Special Forces.

Payne's men had recently been through some heavy fighting. As Montagnards, they fought only for money. If they had all the cash they needed, or the next operation looked particularly hazardous, they did not turn out. When Payne mustered his company, he found he had only 52 men. At full strength it should have had 100. At minimum strength it had to be at least 75 to allow it to operate with three full-strength platoons.

Payne went to a fellow AATTV member, Warrant Officer Jock Stewart, who ran the company that trained Montagnard recruits and scrounged 37 volunteers who had completed just 12 days of training. Now he had three platoons of nearly 30 each. They were under the command Warrant Officer Latham, who also acted a company second-in-command and administrative officer, Sergeant Jack Clement of the USSF, who doubled as radio operator, and Sergeant Gerard Dellwo of the USSF, who was the medical sergeant. The problem was that they barely recognised, let alone knew, the ill-trained troops under their command and they were about to face the best the NVA could fling at them.

The operation began on 18 May, when the battalion was flown to Dac To to begin clearing the road to Ben Het. As they advanced down Route 512, they were shelled and rocketed, but they did not make contact with the enemy directly. Next, they were airlifted forward to a ridgeline 9 kilometres southwest of

Ben Het, 5 kilometres from the Cambodian border, which lay along a likely infiltration route.

On 22 May the 5th MFB were helicoptered into another ridgeline 4 kilometres to the south and took up positions on a hilltop that was pockmarked with craters from an earlier B-52 raid. At 1600, the 1st MFB joined it on an adjoining crest, some 800 metres high. The hilltops were wide enough to dig trenches. They afforded good fields of fire over edges that plunged hundreds of metres into the valleys below, which were choked with primary jungle, bamboo thickets, vines and ferns.

That night orders came that they were to carry out company clearing patrols the following day to locate the 66th NVA regiment. First thing in the morning, US aircraft strafed the areas thought likely to conceal the enemy with 'prophylactic fire'. This tactic is sometimes known euphemistically as 'reconnaissance by fire'.

Tolley's company were first out. As they moved down the ridge, they ran straight into heavy fire. Suffering casualties, the Montagnards quickly retreated to the defensive position. Montez's men were the next to try. They reached 25 metres past where Tolley had been halted. They, too, were pushed back by heavy fire. It seems that the 1st MFB had inadvertently landed on the same ridgeline occupied by the 66th NVA.

New orders came through from Pleiku. The 1st MFB were not longer to hold the 66th NVA until reinforcements arrived. Now, with the support of the 5th MFB, they were to force the 66th NVA off the ridge. Because the top of the ridge was only 200 metres across, with a steep slope on each side, there was no alternative to making a frontal assault with the weaker MFC attacking the superior force of the NVA. In an effort to even up the odds, the morning of the 24th was given over to airstrikes.

At 1430, the 1st MFB began to advance. Payne's company was on the left; Montez's on the right. The ridge was wide enough for only one platoon to be stretched across the front of each company, with the other two following in single file behind. Progress was slow, not because of enemy action but because of the felled trees and craters left by the airstrikes. Tolley's company followed up in the rear. They made even slower progress as they collected weapons and bagged dead bodies for evacuation from the previous day's fighting.

Around 700 metres from the battalion's starting point they spotted the enemy's position on a hilltop. Another airstrike was called in. When it was over, Payne and Montez occupied the hill with Tolley some 150 metres behind down the ridge. There was no one there. The hilltop was 120 metres by 300 metres, cleared of vegetation by the repeated airstrikes and featureless except for the enemy's abandoned trenches and weapons pits.

Far from being destroyed or demoralised by the airstrikes, the NVA had simply pulled back into the cover of the jungle to allow the MFC to occupy the exposed hilltop. After twenty minutes, they began firing mortars, rockets and machine guns from three sides on the Montagnards, who had not had time to dig foxholes. Then the NVA moved into the gap between Tolley and the two lead companies. Unable to break through, Tolley pulled back to defensive positions some 200 metres down the ridge.

Payne tried to manoeuvre his two forward platoons to make

an attack on the machine guns, but they could advance only 15 metres. The enemy were too strong for them. Payne then provided covering fire for Montez, who would do no better.

The position now seemed hopeless and Payne was afraid that his men would break and flee – which would lead to a massacre. He began running from position to position around the perimeter, lobbing grenades, firing his M-16 and shouting encouragement to his men. Payne was next to his radio operator when a rocket-propelled grenade took the man's head off and blew the Armalite from Payne's hands. So he picked up an M-60 and continued the fight. Soon, blood was pouring down his face from a wound on the crown.

In the face of Payne's determined actions, the NVA faltered. Then they reinforced, bringing down the withering fire of at least four machine guns. Under such fire, even seasoned troops might break. The Montagnards began streaming from the ridge down into the valley in panic. Payne arranged covering fire, then dashed across the exposed hilltop to stem the disorderly retreat. He managed to regroup and form a temporary defensive perimeter in the valley some 350 metres from the ridge.

Payne was now wounded by mortar and rocket fragments in the hands and arms, as well as the scalp. Montez had been hit and lay badly injured on the hilltop. Latham, James and Lieutenant Forbes, the US artillery co-ordinator, had also been hit. Many Montagnards had been killed and wounded. Others were unaccounted for.

Two helicopter gunships moved in. Payne directed their fire onto the enemy positions, telling them not to fire directly on the hilltop to avoid hitting the wounded or Tolley's men, who were now slowly pulling back along with ridge to the 5th MFB.

As night began to fall, Payne approached Lieutenant James and told him that he intended to make his way through enemy lines back onto the hilltop, find Sergeant Montez and bring back as many wounded and stragglers as he could find. Payne insisted that he go alone. The only other unwounded adviser was Dellwo, and he was needed to take care of the wounded as well as supervise the defensive position. Payne did not feel that he could trust any of the Montagnards. He could not speak their language and trying to communicate with them in the dark risked giving their position away. James could see that he could not dissuade Payne, but imagined that it was the last he would see of the brave Australian.

With his face and hands caked with blood, Payne set out with an M-16 and a radio. He was helped by the bright moonlight, and the thinning vegetation around the crest gave him visibility of about 6 metres. Every so often, he saw the shadowy figure of an enemy moving about. Then there would be a shot. They were killing the wounded. In all, Payne made four trips through enemy lines that night.

On the first, miraculously, he found Montez, and with a handful of Montagnards he had rounded up managed to get him off the hill. This was all the more dangerous now that he was not alone. Payne himself helped carry Montez, the Montagnards carrying and dragging other wounded. Once he had got them down to the remnants of the battalion in the valley, Payne set out again to see if he could rescue more Montagnards. Each time he collected a handful, he deposited them at a collection point halfway down the hill and went back for more.

On one trip, he was so exhausted that he stopped behind a log to light up a cigarette. It was a foolish thing to do, but somehow it helped. In the darkness, he could hear the NVA on their radio. They were using his name. Once, he was fired on by a group with two machine guns and two AK-47s, but they missed and he slipped away into the gloom.

After three hours' searching, Payne had collected a group of more than thirty and led them down to the defensive position in the valley, only to find that the rest of the battalion had gone. James had decided that he could not wait for Payne. Any one of the shots he heard from the hilltop may, for all he knew, have done for him. James could not afford to wait until daybreak. He had to use the cover of night to get back to the 5th MFB if his men were to stand a chance. A little way down the trail, he found that the wounded were slowing their progress. He left them with Dellwo, saying that if he made it back he would organise their rescue later.

Finding the defensive position deserted, Payne spotted a trail of phosphorous leaf mould that had been overturned by recent passers-by and he decided to follow it. After 200 metres he stumbled upon Dellwo and his party of wounded.

'How he found us I'll never know,' said Dellwo. 'He said he followed our trail of phosphorous glowing in the dark… He insisted that the NVA would find us as he did, if not soon, then in the morning. Also, he wasn't convinced that help would be able to arrive. From past experience with Warrant Officer Payne, I know he had about the coolest head when things seem to be the worst. Despite all that had happened, he had his interpreter, his radio man, all his gear, 40 Montagnards, and he had found us.'

Payne radioed for medevac helicopters, only to be told that none were available. His party, now swelled by fresh wounded, had around a kilometre to cover through enemy-held territory at night. They were forced to stick to the valleys, which were choked with undergrowth and slippery underfoot. Travelling in single file, they made slow and noisy progress, and expected to get fired at by the enemy every step of the way. Montez was a heavy man and Payne and the two medical sergeants took turns carrying him. He continued to radio requests for a medevac chopper. Montez was now dying, the medical sergeants reported. Finally, a helicopter was available, but, while they waited under a hole in the jungle canopy for the chopper to lower its rig, Montez died. They wrapped him in a ground sheet and hid his body in the hope that they would be able to recover it later.

As the journey continued, a small propeller-drive aircraft flew overhead, drowning the sounds of their movements. At last, Payne saw sparks and the sound of one of Tolley's mortar parties in the 5th Battalion area. At 0310 on 25 May Payne brought his party of wounded in. He had been in action continuously for over twelve hours and the resuce he had pulled off was little short of miraculous.

Otherwise, the operation had been a disaster. Of the original 89 in his company, only 31 survived, many of them wounded. In all, the 1st MFB lost 50 per cent killed or missing. They were withdrawn from operations, re-equipped and retrained, then returned to action under Australian command.

In September 1969, Payne was called to a meeting at the Free

World Building in Saigon. There, the Australian commander in Vietnam, Major General Hay, made a surprise announcement. Payne had been awarded the Victoria Cross. Fortunately, his close friend 'Simmo' Simpson, who had received the same shock news only a few weeks before, was on hand with advice.

'Take is easy and get a few beers down you,' he said.

Typically, Payne was modest about his achievement. 'I went out on my own and picked up a few blokes and hauled then in – someone had to go out,' he said. 'You don't set out to win a Victoria Cross. And, believe me, you certainly don't go back looking for another one.'

On other occasions he was more reflective.

'I think it's the conscious responsibility you assume for other men's lives,' he said, 'the moral obligation you have towards your soldiers. Your instinct is to be a survivor, but your instinct also demands that your soldiers survive as well... You just do what you have to do. You do it without the luxury of thinking, will I or won't I?'

It was part of the brotherhood of the fighting man.

'In war we are closer than blood brothers,' he said. 'There is nothing closer than those you have felt and smelt the full horror of war with... You have to feel it, smell the carnage, the death, the horror and the noise... my God, the noise. Only the men who have been there can know it, it's that terrible, that horrible.'

Soon after, Payne was sent home to Brisbane for treatment for a duodenal ulcer that had been diagnosed while his wounds were being tended. Although he was warmly received in military circles, the antiwar movement was now in full cry in Australia and Payne did not like what he saw. There were no more parades for returning soldiers. Veterans were ignored or openly abused. He found he could not go anywhere in his uniform, even though he had won the VC.

'My kids had to fight their way through school in Canberra,' he said, 'where the kids of the public servants told them their old man was a murderer.'

On his recovery, he was posted as an instructor at the Royal Military College, Duntroon, remaining until he joined the 42nd Battalion of the Royal Queensland Regiment at Mackay, Queensland, on 20 December 1972.

'I went into action with 272 bullets and eight hand grenades and came out with a VC,' he told colleagues.

He was presented with his Victoria Cross by the Queen aboard the royal yacht *Britannia* at Brisbane on 13 April 1970. The citation read:

Keith Payne was born at Ingham, Queensland, on 30 August 1933, the son of Henry Thomas Payne. He was educated at Ingham state school and then apprenticed as a cabinetmaker. On 13 August 1951 he enlisted in the regular army, after a short period in the CMF [Commonwealth Military Force], and was posted to the 1st Battalion, the Royal Australian Regiment, in September 1952. He served in Korea with the 1st Battalion from April 1952 until March 1953, then the 28th British Commonwealth Infantry Brigade Defence and Employment Platoon, and returned to Queensland in September where he married

Florence Catherine Plaw, of the WRAAC [Women's Royal Australian Army Corps], on 5 December 1954.

Periods with the 4th Cadet and the 11th National Service Training Battalions followed, and on 17 February 1960 he joined the 3rd Battalion. He accompanied the 3rd to Malaya, was promoted to sergeant on 1 June 1961 and in February 1965 joined the 5th Battalion; promotion to temporary warrant officer class II came on 4 June 1965. The following June he went as company sergeant major to the Officer Training Unit and from February 1967 until March 1968 served in Papua New Guinea with the 2nd Pacific Islands Regiment. He was posted to Headquarters Northern Command at Brisbane prior to being appointed to the Training Team in Vietnam on 24 February 1969.

Payne soon joined a mobile strike force battalion, which was reconnoitring enemy infiltration routes from Laos into Vietnam. Once the routes were located they were interdicted in an attempt to relieve the pressure on the recently constructed and occupied Ben Het Special Forces camp.

On 24 May Payne was commanding the 212th Company of the 1st Mobile Strike Force Battalion when the battalion was attacked by a numerically superior North Vietnamese force. The two forward companies were heavily attacked with rockets, mortars and machineguns from three directions simultaneously. The indigenous soldiers faltered so Payne rushed about firing his Armalite rifle and hurling grenades to keep the enemy at bay while he tried to rally the soldiers. In doing so he was wounded in the hands, upper arm and hip by four pieces of rocket shrapnel and one piece of mortar shrapnel.

The battalion commander decided to fight his way back to base and this movement commenced by the only available route. With a few remnants of his company, which had suffered heavy casualties, Payne covered the withdrawal with grenades and gunfire and then attempted to round up more of his company. By nightfall he had succeeded in gathering a composite party of his own and another company and had established a small defensive perimeter, about 350 metres north-east of the hill. The enemy by now had captured the former hilltop position.

In darkness Payne set off to locate those who had been cut off and disoriented. At 9 p.m. he crawled over to one displaced group, having tracked them by the fluorescence of their footsteps in rotting vegetable matter on the ground, and thus began an 800-metre traverse of the area for the next three hours. The enemy were moving about and firing, but Payne was able to locate some 40 men, some wounded, some of whom Payne personally dragged out. He organised others who were not wounded to crawl out on their stomachs with wounded on their backs.

Once he concentrated his party he navigated them back to the temporary perimeter only to find the position abandoned by troops who had moved back to the battalion base. Undeterred, he led his party, as well as another group of wounded encountered en route, back to the battalion base where they arrived at about 3 a.m.

His sustained and heroic personal efforts in this action were outstanding and undoubtedly saved the lives of his indigenous soldiers and several of his fellow advisers.

The United States awarded him the Distinguished Service Cross and the Silver Star, while the Republic of Vietnam honoured him with its Cross of Gallantry with bronze star. His photograph and citation are displayed in the Hall of Heroes at the John F Kennedy Center for Military Assistance, Fort Bragg, North Carolina. He was made a freeman of the city of Brisbane and the shire of Hinchinbrook, and a park in the Brisbane suburb of Stafford, where he lived at the time of his decoration, was named Keith Payne Park in July 1971. His portrait was painted for the Australian War Memorial by Stanley Bourne.

Payne left the army on 31 March 1975. He then signed a three-year contract to serve in the army of the Sultan of Oman with the rank of captain during the Dhofar war. Although the British Army seconded officers and men for this campaign, Payne as an Australian had to go there in a private capacity. When a pressman at the airport accused the most decorated Australian soldier of being a mercenary, Payne could hardly contain his rage.

'A mercenary is a man who would fight without principle for monetary gain,' he spat back. 'I don't have to go to Oman for monetary reasons. I could be sitting on a beach at Bucasia. But the Australian government won't allow Australian soldiers to fight Communists. So, as a soldier, I'm going to fight them the best way I can.'

As far as Payne was concerned, he was going to do in Dhofar

the same thing he had done during his entire career – in Korea, in Malaya, in Borneo and in Vietnam – and that was fight Communism, this time in the form of the Popular Front for the Liberation of Oman, who were backed by the Soviet Union, the People's Republic of China and Oman's avowedly Marxist neighbour the People's Democratic Republic of Yemen. Communism spreading through Asia, many still felt, was a threat to his homeland.

'I am tremendously worried about the future of Australia,' he said.

But, after six months in Oman, he returned to Australia. Perhaps finding that fighting in the Gulf was not the same as fighting in East Asia, he broke his contract and stayed at home.

'I was fearful that the next time I wouldn't perform,' he told a magazine. 'When you're a commanding officer, you are judge and jury and men's lives depend on you. It's not the fire-fight you're afraid of, but the fear of making mistakes and costing lives.'

It became clear to those around him that Vietnam had deeply affected him. He had irrational outbursts of rage, which he called 'brainoes' – perhaps a symptom of post-traumatic stress.

'There's a lot of blokes like me suffering from this stress thing,' he said. 'It's your nerves, like metal fatigue.'

Eventually he had to give up his civilian job as a salesman and went into retirement on a war-service disability pension.

PART IV
THE FALKLANDS

On 2 April, Argentina, under the military junta of General Leopoldo Galtieri, invaded the Falklands, claiming that the islands – which they call *Las Malvinas* – were their territory. By the end of the month, Argentina had stationed more than ten thousand men, mostly poorly trained conscripts but also marines and special forces units, on the Falkland Islands and their dependencies. This move made the repressive Argentine government briefly popular with its own citizens. Thousands turned out in the Plaza de Mayo in front of the Presidential Palace to demonstrate their support.

Although the Falkland Islands are 8,000 miles from Britain, the British government under Margaret Thatcher declared a 200-mile exclusion zone around them and sent a large naval and military task force. The sinking of the Argentine cruiser, the

General Belgrano – a former American vessel and a survivor of the Japanese attack on Pearl Harbor in 1941 – outside the exclusion zone kept other Argentine warships well away. But the Argentine Air Force, armed with French-built Exocet anti-ship missiles, destroyed a significant amount of British shipping, including the destroyer HMS *Sheffield* and the *Atlantic Conveyor*. However, they could not prevent a British amphibious landing near San Carlos on East Falkland on 21 May.

From there, the British struck out against Argentine forces to the south, taking Darwin and Goose Green. They then turned eastwards, fighting key battles around Port Stanley in early June and taking the capital on the 14th. The South Sandwich Islands were retaken on 20 June.

In all, some 11,400 Argentine prisoners of war were taken, all of whom were released soon after. Nearly 750 Argentine men were killed – including 368 on board the *General Belgrano* – while the British lost 256. Two VCs were awarded during the action.

Their humiliating defeat discredited the military junta and civilian government was restored in Argentina the following year. Victory in the Falklands War gave the formerly unpopular Margaret Thatcher a landslide victory in the 1983 general election in Britain.

CHAPTER NINE

'SUNRAY IS DOWN'

LIEUTENANT COLONEL HERBERT JONES

28 May 1982, commanding 2nd Battalion, Parachute Regiment (Posthumous)

Lieutenant Colonel 'H' Jones was the commander of 2 Para during the Falklands War. He led his men into the first major battle at Goose Green on 27 May 1982 and was killed leading an attack on an Argentine machine-gun post near Darwin. No one who knew him was the least bit surprised.

Born Herbert Jones in Putney on 14 May 1940, he was the son of an artist and a nurse. At Eton, he became a keen sportsman with a passion for physical fitness that remained with him throughout his service career. He sailed, skied and rowed for the college. Jones disliked the named Herbert and, throughout his life, clung to the nickname 'H'.

In boyhood, Jones had also developed a passion for all things military. He was a keen war-gamer and never wanted any career other than the army. On leaving Eton, he went to the Royal Military School at Sandhurst as an officer cadet. In July 1960, he was commissioned into the Devon and Dorset Regiment, an infantry regiment, where he took up motor racing. In the regiment he gained a reputation as being an 'action man' – an officer who led from the front and who believed that setting an example was the best way to lead men.

After five years with the Devon and Dorsets, he was seconded into the 3rd Battalion of the Parachute Regiment, where he commanded a mortar platoon. Over the next fourteen years he moved up the ranks through a series of regimental and staff postings. He became adjutant of his battalion, a junior staff officer at the headquarters of the United Kingdom Land Forces (UKLF), a student at Camberley Staff College, a company commander, a brigade major in Northern Ireland, where he was made an MBE, and an instructor at the School of Infantry in Warminster, Wiltshire. In June 1979, he was promoted to lieutenant colonel and he took up a senior staff post back at the UKLF, where he was awarded an OBE for his part in planning the deployment of a peacekeeping force in Zimbabwe in the run-up to independence. Then, in April 1982, he finally realised his ambition and was appointed commanding officer of the 2nd Battalion of the Parachute Regiment – the legendary 2 Para.

The battalion had suffered the loss of sixteen men in an IRA ambush at Warrenpoint in Northern Ireland on 27 August 1979. However, it still had a sound staff structure and experienced NCOs. Jones rebuilt morale and moulded 2 Para into a formidable fighting force with a zest for soldiering plainly inspired by his own. He was an advocate of physical fitness and shooting, and was known for his uncompromising approach. But he did have his humorous side. Once, while on a training exercise in Kenya, he pointed out an imaginary bunker on a hill to a soldier who was carrying a 66mm anti-tank rocket launcher and told the man to take it out – and quickly. He put such pressure on the hapless man that he grew flustered. When his CO yelled in exasperation, the man loosed off a round. The rocket sailed clean over the hilltop and exploded in the distance on the other side.

'Christ,' said 'H', 'he's missed the fucking mountain.'

He was known for his impatience, and his wife Sara said that, when they played board games at home – usually war games – he would move other people's pieces to speed up play. On exercises he would be found with the lead section, often out in front, urging everyone on. On several such occasions, the umpires ruled him 'dead' because of the exposed position he put himself in. This was all too prescient.

When Argentina invaded the Falkland Islands in 1982 and Britain responded by sending a task force, Jones cut short a skiing holiday to rush to the Ministry of Defence to persuade the authorities that 2 Para must go. His wife maintains that he would have been impossible to live with if he had not succeeded in getting to the Falklands. His battalion became part of the 3rd Commando Brigade, an elite formation under Brigadier Thompson of the Royal Marines.

On 21 May 1982 – D-Day – 2 Para landed at Blue Beach in

Bonners Bay off San Carlos Water. They had been taught the basics of an amphibious assault on the way by the Royal Marines. That did not stop the Paras calling the landing craft 'rubbish skips' and an amphibious assault 'rubbish skipping'. After hitting the beaches, they moved south on foot to Sussex Mountain, where they dug in to protect the southern flank of 3 Brigade. A large Argentine force was known to be based south of San Carlos at Darwin and Goose Green and it presented a real threat to the men at San Carlos.

In preparation for action Colonel 'H' Jones and his second-in-command, Major Chris Keeble, reorganised the battalion. A command-and-control structure was produced for 2 Para that would enable Jones to move freely among his men with a small staff and signallers. Keeble had a skeleton staff that duplicated Jones's tactical HQ. Then there was an HQ company separate from the main HQ. This structure relieved the colonel and his second-in-command of routine administration.

The officer commanding the HQ company was in charge of ammunition and casualty evacuation. He and the main HQ were responsible for following the way the battle was developing and moving ammunition forward as it was needed. The main HQ also had the officer commanding the support company with its mortars and anti-tank weapons. He was also responsible for artillery and air support. The adjutant handled the administration for the colonel, while a regimental sergeant major took care of ammunition resupply and the evacuation of prisoners of war. All this allowed 'H' to concentrate on the battle as it developed from the front lines.

A unique intelligence-gathering organisation was also instituted. 2 Para had a patrol company that comprised a four-man foot patrol, a vehicle-borne team and an observation post. They worked closely with the intelligence officer, who passed information direct to the colonel.

'H' also instituted a new procedure for passing orders to the company commanders. He would hold what the SAS called a 'Chinese parliament', where he would talk through the various attack and defence options with all the officers commanding the rifle and support companies. Everyone had a chance to air his views and point out problems or hazards of the various different courses of action. By the end of the discussion, everyone had a good idea of what lay ahead. Then the colonel prepared his orders. As a result, there were no surprises when orders arrived and the company commanders had a clear idea of what was expected of them.

2 Para were well armed for the task that awaited them. Before the Falklands they had been earmarked to go to Belize. They had already drawn their jungle-training weapons, so they were equipped with twice the normal number of machine guns, American M-16 Armalite automatic rifles and M-79 grenade launchers.

From the heights of Sussex Mountain, they dominated the southern approaches to the San Carlos beachhead and could observe any attempts made by the Argentine forces to counterattack from Darwin and Goose Green. Patrols were sent out, but reconnaissance activities by Special Forces limited their range. This was particularly frustrating for the patrol company, who were held back behind a screen of the SAS, SBS and the Arctic Warfare Cadre.

On the night of the landings at San Carlos, the SAS had staged a raid on Goose Green. Approaching overland, they poured in a heavy volume of automatic and anti-tank fire, convincing the Argentine garrison that they were under attack from a much larger force. This dissuaded them from investigating what was going on at San Carlos. 2 Para were to have followed up, but Argentine air attacks took their toll of shipping. HMS *Coventry* was sunk and the converted Cunard container ship *Atlantic Conveyor* was hit by an Exocet missile with the loss of three heavy-lift Chinooks and six Wessex helicopters on board.

Without transport, 2 Para's attack on Darwin and Goose Green was cancelled. In fact, Brigadier Julian Thompson, head of 3 Commando Brigade, believed that an attack on the Argentine forces there was not necessary. He thought they could be quarantined so that they could not move across the isthmus that connects Goose Green to the rest of East Falkland. But 'H' Jones was adamant that an attack was necessary and argued his case forcefully. His argument was that, as the task force's plan was to move from west to east across East Falklands to attack Port Stanley 50 miles away across open terrain, any force left in the rear was a real threat.

The argument did not win the day, but, after six days with the brigade sitting in its positions around Ajax bay, the military planners and the public at home in the UK wanted action. The Argentine forces at Goose Green were close at hand and presented the only opportunity for a spectacular victory to kick off the campaign. Now 2 Para were ordered to attack Darwin and Goose Green.

SAS patrols reported that the area was held in approximately battalion strength – five hundred men reinforced by some artillery, three anti-aircraft batteries and engineers. This gave 2 Para a ratio of 1:1 in infantrymen. According to the military manuals, to attack a defended position, you needed a ratio of 3:1 to give a reasonable chance for success. In fact, the position was much worse that this. After the SAS had made their reports, the Argentine forces there had been reinforced by men from 12 Regiment on Mount Kent, swelling their numbers to 1,400.

While Colonel 'H' Jones has often been criticised for being unnecessarily gung-ho, he was not happy with making a frontal assault down a long narrow peninsula, leaving him no room to manoeuvre or make flanking attacks. He suggested that they make an airborne attack at night. This was vetoed because of the shortage of helicopters and few of the pilots had been trained with the new night-vision equipment. Nor could he make a new amphibious assault, flanking the Argentines. The sea there was full of thick seaweed or kelp that would snag the landing crafts' propellers. There were hidden rocks and the problems of navigating in confined waters at night to consider. It was reckoned that, in any seaborne landing, only 50 per cent of the landing craft would make it ashore. There was no alternative: 2 Para were going to have to make a frontal assault on foot. This would take them across exposed ground, where they would be open to small-arms, mortar and artillery fire, as well as to air attack by Pucaras, Argentine ground-attack planes. But 'H' believed that, if they made a night attack, the Paras' speed and aggressiveness would overwhelm the defences and, if they kept moving forward, hitting hard, Argentinian resistance would crumble.

Last light was at 1615 and first light was at 0630. That would give the Paras fourteen hours of darkness to move from the assembly area at Camilla Creek House to the high ground overlooking Darwin, 8 kilometres away, then on to Goose Green, another 2 kilometres beyond that. This could be done only if they left much of their heavy equipment behind and depended on the Royal Navy and other units for fire support.

Two patrols from 2 Para confirmed that the enemy positions straddled the northern end of the isthmus, just south of Darwin. They were particularly strong on Darwin Hill, which overlooks the town. The patrols withdrew when they came under enemy fire.

Jones came up with a detailed plan of attack that would take place over a night and a day and had six distinct phases. It began with a naval bombardment by HMS *Arrow*, supported by artillery fire from the three guns of 8 Battery of 29 Commando Battery of the Royal Artillery and two of 2 Para's 81mm heavy mortars. The aim was to defeat the enemy during the hours of darkness, so that the Paras could identify and liberate the civilian population in daylight.

At first light, the battalion's mopping-up operations would be supported by Scout helicopters carrying air-to-surface SS-11 missiles as well as Harrier jump jets in a ground-attack role. For air defence they would have two detachments armed with Blowpipe surface-to-air missiles proved by the 4th Regiment of the Royal Artillery and the Royal Marines.

On the night of 26 May, 2 Para would leave Sussex Mountain.

They would lie up during the day and attack on the night of the 27th. When they started out, the weather was atrocious. There was a cutting wind and driving rain. To save his men from this misery, 'H' Jones took the calculated risk of letting the entire battalion squeeze into Camilla Creek House and its outbuildings. Bringing all his men together made them vulnerable, but he figured that under concealment they would safe and if they got some decent rest out of the weather it would save casualties the next night.

Then came the bad news. At around noon on 27 May, they turned on the BBC World Service only to be told that the 'parachute battalion is poised and ready to assault Darwin and Goose Green'. Now the enemy knew they were coming. Jones cursed the government and the Ministry of Defence, convinced that they were the source of the leak.

'I'll sue the lot,' he said.

Although 3 Brigade's orders were merely to raid Darwin and Goose Green, Jones was not a man for half-measures and opted for an all-out full-battalion attack. It began at 0230 on 28 May 1982. HMS *Arrow* fired on the first line of the enemy positions and the support company moved south to establish a position overlooking the enemy's flank.

First contact with the enemy came when the Paras left the area of Camilla Creek House to the north of the isthmus. Harassing fire from Argentine 105-Pack howitzers fell along the likely lines of advance.

At first light the Paras captured a four-man Argentine patrol that had driven up in a blue-and-white Land Rover the

Argentinians had commandeered in Goose Green. This was a standing patrol that covered the tracks from Burntside House and Darwin up to Camilla Creek. Captain Rod Bell of the Royal Marines, a Spanish-speaking officer attached to 2 Para for the operation, questioned the two uninjured men. The officer, Lieutenant Morales, was a professional and would give little away. The other man, Private Pedro Galva, was more talkative, but knew little. The other two men had tried to escape and had been wounded. One of them, a sergeant, had a round through the legs. The regimental medical officer, Captain Steve Hughes of the Royal Army Medical Corps, said that he was relieved that the first battle casualties he had had to treat were Argentine.

The main assault began at 0235 when A Company moved against Burntside House. They were already 35 minutes behind schedule. The buildings were raked with fire, setting fire to the outhouses, and, although the battalion had been told that there were no civilians outside Darwin and Goose Green, they were surprised to find that a family of four kelpers, including a grandmother of eighty, had survived the onslaught. The Argentine platoon there withdrew and their artillery fire began to drop across the neck of the isthmus.

Having secured their left flank, 2 Para cleared the land to the northwest of Burntside Pond. B Company crossed their start line at 0710 and cleared the positions on the high ground to the west of the pond. In Colonel Jones's plan, D Company would pass through B Company and continue south, but they came under small-arms fire from enemy positions that had been bypassed by

B Company. So they engaged the enemy and cleared the positions. This delayed them.

While this fighting was in progress, A Company moved south past Coronation Point, a small promontory north of Darwin, at 0515. There was only 75 minutes left before dawn and 2 Para were far from their objectives. B Company had been halted by enemy fire 1,000 metres north of Boca House, while D Company were 3,500 metres (3,830 yards) from Goose Green. Only A Company were within striking distance of their objective, Darwin. The problem was that A Company, who had moved almost unmolested through the night, were so far ahead of the rest of the battalion that any further advance would require a major change of plan. The company commander, Major Dair Farrar-Hockley radioed for instructions. Jones told him to stay where he was until he could reach him as assess the situation.

When he arrived, 'H' urged an immediate advance. It was now 0630. 2 Para, who had been winning their actions at night, would now have to face their well-dug-in enemy in daylight. Leaving a platoon at Coronation Point to give them covering fire, the other two platoons hooked round the small bay to attack Darwin from the west. To their right was a 100-foot hill on whose southern slopes was Boca House, which B Company should have taken some hours before.

As dawn broke, the battalion realised that, during the hours of darkness, they had only brushed against a screen. The main force was still intact. During the bombardment, HMS *Arrow*'s Mark 8 4.5-inch gun had malfunctioned, so that she had been unable to provide the weight of gunfire Colonel Jones's plan had called for.

She left at dawn. Winds blowing across the isthmus made accurate artillery shelling difficult and mist at sea prevented the Harriers giving support. Argentine artillery fire was still falling between the forward British troops and their resupply of ammunition. But the Paras found unused boxes of 7.62mm rifle bullets in captured trenches and began helping themselves. They were now very much on their own.

Some 1,500 yards to the north of Darwin Hill, the main HQ and Regimental Air Post, along with Defence Platoon, Robert Fox of the BBC and David Norris of the *Daily Mail* were digging in when they came under fire from mortars and artillery. Captain Hughes now had his hands full with British and Argentine casualties, while the RSM, Malcolm Simpson, was dealing with a trickle of prisoners.

Meanwhile, Jones and his tactical HQ were moving down the track that led to the front of Darwin Hill behind A Company, who were just about to attack Port Darwin when they came under heavy machine-gun fire from positions to the west. There was nothing for it. They would now have to clear the positions on Darwin Hill with their machine guns and 66mm rocket launchers. Two machine guns from each section hammered away at the Argentine positions until they stopped shooting back. The anti-tank rocket launchers also went into action. This was a dangerous operation, as the operator had to kneel with his head and chest exposed to aim at the Argentine bunkers. Nevertheless, the weapon was very effective. The blast alone could kill an enemy without leaving any marks.

Darwin Hill was cut with two gullies or re-entrants, the larger of which was filled with thick clumps of gorse. 2 Platoon, under Lieutenant Mark Coe, were ordered to advance up the gully and take the hill. Advancing almost unopposed to start with, Coe found himself confronted by the main line of the Argentines' defence. The entire Argentine 12th Regiment opened fire and 2 Platoon, with 1 Platoon following, tried to take cover in the gully, under withering fire and taking heavy casualties. They threw smoke grenades. These set the gorse on fire, only adding to the confusion. For the next two-and-a-half hours, the two platoons were pinned down by a series of well-sited Argentine positions. The machine guns were positioned to fire in interlocking arcs, so that, when men moved forward to engage one, they came under fire from another. These machine-gun emplacements had been so well constructed and camouflaged that they had not been seen by the SAS reconnaissance patrols.

B Company were also stalled. They found it impossible to move down the forward slope facing Boca House under intense mortar and machine-gun fire and were driven back over the crest. 2 Para were now in a dangerously exposed position. Their two lead companies were on open ground in front of heavily defended positions and were taking heavy casualties. They had lost their naval support. The 81mm mortars and 105s were running low on ammunition. The Harriers still could not take off and the rifle companies, the battalion HQ and the gun line were vulnerable to attack from Pucaras that might take off from Port Stanley at any time.

Major Neame, commanding D Company, suggested moving down the western shoreline, outflanking the enemy to the right.

This was the move that would win the battle some time later. But Jones would not hear of it.

'Don't tell me how to run my battle,' he snapped over the radio.

Jones himself had to take shelter from the heavy fire. But now he decided that he ought to be up front with A Company.

'Come on, we can't stay here all day,' he said to his tactical headquarters.

They ran, crouched and crawled for some 300 metres until they reached the end of the inlet, which was still some 200 metres from A Company. Between there and the gully was a stand of gorse that offered protection from the enemy's gaze if not from their gunfire. They forced their way through it, only to find that there was another 100 metres of open ground before the gorse in the gully offered similar protection.

They divided into two groups. Sergeant Norman threw a smoke grenade and, under its cover, the first group raced across. A Company's sergeant major threw another and took a second group across without casualty. Soon after, Jones and his tactical HQ flopped down beside Farrar-Hockley within 60 metres of the enemy trenches.

'What the hell is happening?' he asked. 'And what are you doing about it?'

Farrar-Hockley, who won the MC for his actions that day, was not best pleased to have his commanding officer breathing down his neck under these circumstances, especially as Jones had held up his advance during the hours of darkness. He explained that he still could not raise an airstrike and the artillery would not lay down a barrage, since his men were too close to the enemy. The wind was between 50 and 60 knots and could easily bring the shells down on their own positions. In the noise, smoke and confusion, it was difficult to rally orders, but his men were concentrating their fire on the nearby trenches and there had been some close-quarters fighting. If their ammunition held out, they would chip away at the defences and, eventually, force the enemy to surrender. In the meantime, they could expect heavy casualties from the defensive positions overlooking them.

Jones was faced with two equally unpleasant alternatives: he could bring up reinforcements in the shape of C and D Companies, but there was no guarantee that they could get through; or he could withdraw A Company, which would involve heavy losses. Neither alternative was acceptable.

For Jones it was important to maintain the impetus of the attack. The Paras were very exposed, but, if they did not keep moving forward, they would suffer greater casualties. So he asked Coe whether he could make his way up to the gorse at the top of the gully with a mortar officer. Coe said he thought he could, though it would be a bit 'hairy'. But Farrar-Hockley had already tried this, without success, so the plan was abandoned.

Jones then told Farrar-Hockley to organise an attack on the summit. Unwilling to send others on such a dangerous mission, Farrar-Hockley led a small party of fifteen to twenty that included the adjutant, Captain David Wood, and the company second-in-command, Captain Chris Dent, up the hill. Laying down smoke, they raced up the slope after him, but were met with intense machine-gun and rifle fire. Then the strong wind blew the smoke away. Wood and Dent, along with Corporal

Hardman, were shot dead and Farrar-Hockley had no choice but to retreat.

Jones had witnessed this assault and turned to Sergeant Norman, his personal escort, and the others and yelled, 'Follow me, we're going right.'

It was around 0900 and Mark Coe recalled Jones's parting words: 'Come on, A Company, get your skirts off.' Under the circumstances this did not go down very well.

Jones ran to his right down the gully, then swung left up the smaller cut in the hope that he could outflank the defences.

'He was 100 per cent aware of what faced him round that corner, and no one can detract from his own personal bravery,' said Coe.

Although he was now 42, Jones was still incredibly fit and was soon 25 metres ahead of the others. As he reached the second gully, Norman could see the colonel starting up the slope.

'Watch out, there's enemy to your left,' someone shouted.

Norman saw a trench and, as the Argentinians opened up, he dived for cover. He loosed off an entire magazine – twenty rounds – then fumbled for another one. Major Tony Rice saw the trench.

'H' ran at it firing his SMG [Sterling machine gun] and then rolled down the slope,' he said, 'changed his magazine and then ran back at the trench again.'

Then Norman spotted another trench higher up on the right-hand side of the gully.

'Watch your back,' he yelled at Jones.

But Jones continued his climb towards the left-hand trench

regardless. Norman opened up in support. As Jones approached the left-hand trench, the one to his rear opened fire. Bullets kicked up dirt all around him. Then a bullet hit him in the small of the back. He fell forwards towards the first trench. There were two Argentinians in it. One was wounded. The other one stood up and tried to finish 'H' off, but as he raised his rifle he realised that he was dangerously exposed.

Norman was just 25 metres from Jones, but there was no way he could reach him. All he could do was keep on firing. The others then began to catch up. Eventually Corporal Abols came forward with a 66mm rocket launcher and blasted the right-hand trench.

'He fired another at the next and hit that, too,' said Coe. 'That I think was the last straw that broke the camel's back. At that point they started coming out, having lost probably six trenches by this stage. At last we were on top of the spur, and then all of a sudden the whole thing just collapsed… people were putting their hands up and coming out of their holes.'

Soon the hill was awash with white flags as the other positions quickly surrendered.

With the fighting over, Sergeant Norman and Major Rice made their way forward to the colonel, who was barely conscious. They removed his webbing and turned him over.

'He had been lying alone for about twenty minutes or more,' said Rice, 'but when we got to him he was still just alive… He'd gone a sort of waxy colour and was panting weakly.'

There was little blood but he was deep in shock, indicating that there was considerable internal bleeding.

'It had been drummed into us the importance of getting saline into the wounded,' said Coe. 'We gave him a drip and a half. Then he slipped into unconsciousness.'

To provide any chance of saving his life, it was vital that Jones be evacuated immediately. They radioed for a helicopter. Permission was denied. Another request, couched in more forceful language, was transmitted. This time a Scout was sent.

Norman and the others then made an improvised stretcher to carry Jones to a suitable landing zone. They made it out of a few pieces of wood they had found and a sheet of corrugated iron from a trench. But, when they put 'H' on it, it broke and he fell to the ground. By this time he was unconscious. Eventually they managed to carry Jones up to the top of the spur, where Farrar-Hockley came to see him and reassure Norman that a helicopter was on its way.

Unfortunately, the Scout had been spotted by two Argentine Pucaras, who attacked. The pilot, Lieutenant Richard Nunn of the Royal Marines, was killed outright. The gunner, Sergeant Belcher, survived, but had his right leg amputated above the knee. Nevertheless, another Royal Marine helicopter, piloted by Captain Jeff Niblett, was sent and eventually got through.

Within minutes of being brought to the top of the hill – forty minutes after he had been hit – Jones died. At 0930, the terse transmission went out: 'Sunray is down.'

This was the standard message indicating that the commanding officer had been killed. It alerted Major Chris Keeble that he was now in charge. Soon afterwards, D Company then began their flanking movement. The next day, the

Argentinians capitulated – some 1,400 men, mostly air force personnel, surrendered to 400 Paras.

The battle for Darwin and Goose Green cost 2 Para 16 dead and 35 wounded. The 92 Argentinians defending the ridge alone lost 18 dead and 39 wounded. The Argentines also lost a large cache of canisters filled with napalm, which the Paras found at Goose Green.

Two days later the dead were buried at Ajax Bay. It was a simple ceremony. There was no time to prepare, because there were still battles to be won. There was no bugler or firing party. The commander of Land Forces, Major-General Jeremy Moore of the Royal Marines, and the rest of 2 Para stood around the large grave as the sixteen bodies, wrapped in plastic body bags and each draped with the Union Flag, were placed side by side in the communal grave. As the company saluted, the regimental sergeant major scattered a handful of earth over the dead.

There was some deliberation over whether Colonel 'H' Jones should be awarded the VC. Senior officers were critical of what Jones did in the final moments before he was killed. His critics have claimed that Jones failed in his task of being the overall leader of 2 Para and that he lost sight of the 'big picture', which required him to take a step back and take command of what 2 Para as an entirety was doing, not just A Company. Then there are those who said that Jones believed that his men were in mortal danger while they were pinned down and that he did what came naturally to him: he led from the front. There were even unfounded rumours that, since 'H' Jones had been shot in the back, his own men had killed him for leading them recklessly into danger.

But his commanding officer, Brigadier Thompson, had no doubts. He 'very strongly recommended' Jones for the VC, while the overall commander of the Task Force, Admiral Sir John Fieldhouse, only 'recommended' Jones to the VC committee – no more than that. Whether Jones was doing the job of a commanding officer at the moment he died or not, there can be no doubt about his personal courage, his disregard for danger and his forceful leadership in the field. And on 11 October 1982 – nearly twenty weeks after his death and four months after the end of the Falklands War – 'H' was awarded his VC. When she heard the news, his widow Sara cracked open a bottle of champagne with the family.

'He would have expected it of us,' she said. 'It's a marvellous hour. He knew what was needed and went into action with hesitation. It was typical of 'H'. He always led from the front.'

The citation read:

On 28th May 1982 Lieutenant Colonel Jones was commanding 2nd Battalion, The Parachute Regiment on operations on the Falkland Islands. The battalion was ordered to attack enemy positions in and around the settlements of Darwin and Goose Green. During the attack against an enemy, who was well dug in with mutually supporting positions sited in depth, the battalion was held up just South of Darwin by a particularly well-prepared and resilient enemy position of at least 11 trenches on an important ridge. A number of casualties were received. In order to read the battle fully and ensure that the momentum of his attack was not lost, Colonel Jones took forward his reconnaissance party to the foot of a re-entrant, which a section of his battalion had just secured. Despite persistent, heavy and accurate fire the reconnaissance party gained the top of the re-entrant, at approximately the same time as the enemy positions. However, these had been well prepared and continued to pour effective fire onto the battalion advance, which, by now held up for over an hour and under increasingly heavy artillery fire, was in danger of faltering.

In his effort to gain a good viewpoint, Colonel Jones was now at the very front of his battalion. It was clear to him that desperate measures were needed in order to overcome the enemy position and rekindle the attack, and that unless these measures were taken promptly the battalion would sustain increasing casualties and the attack perhaps even fail. It was time for personal leadership and action. Colonel Jones immediately seized a sub-machine gun, and, calling on those around him and with total disregard for his own safety, charged the nearest enemy position. This action exposed him to fire from a number of trenches.

As he charged up a short slope at the enemy position he was seen to fall and roll backward downhill. He immediately picked himself up, and charged the enemy trench firing his sub-machine gun and seemingly oblivious to the intense fire directed at him. He was hit by fire from another trench, which he outflanked and fell dying only a few feet from the enemy he had assaulted. A short time later a company of the battalion attacked the enemy, who quickly surrendered. The devastating display of courage by Colonel Jones had completely undermined their will to fight further.

Thereafter the momentum of the attack was rapidly regained, Darwin and Goose Green were liberated, and the battalion released the local inhabitants unharmed and forced the surrender of some 1,200 of the enemy.

The achievements of 2nd Battalion, The Parachute Regiment, at Darwin and Goose Green set the tone for the subsequent land victory on the Falklands. They achieved such a moral superiority over the enemy in this first battle, that despite the advantages of numbers and selection of battle-ground, they never thereafter doubted either the superior fighting qualities of the British troops, or their own inevitable defeat. This was an action of the utmost gallantry by a commanding officer whose dashing leadership and courage throughout the battle were an inspiration to all about him.

Farrar-Hockley concurred: 'His inspiration and example were to remain with us for the rest of the campaign,' he said.

Prime Minister Margaret Thatcher took a broader view of Jones's heroic deeds: 'It gave renewed faith to the people of the Falklands and renewed their understanding to all of those who doubted whether we would see it through. We were going to see it through. Our resolve – our total resolve – to reclaim those islands was demonstrated by that one particular deed. It was heroic leadership. It is part of our history. It was heroism and leadership of matchless order, really. There are one or two things in history which have been similar. The bravest of the brave were there that day.'

On 25 October 1982, Jones was one of the fourteen men reburied at Blue Beach Military Cemetery overlooking San Carlos Bay. This time the seven soldiers and seven marines were buried in coffins in individual graves with due ceremony. The 23rd Psalm was sung. A bugler played the 'Last Post' and 'Reveille'. A lone piper played a lament from the shore while a navy launch dropped a wreath on San Carlos waters. The first wreath was laid by Defence Secretary John Nott, one of the people 'H' had threatened to sue. A family wreath was laid by Commander Timothy Jones, 'H''s brother, whose ship happened to be in the Falklands at the time.

It has long been the tradition that British servicemen are buried in the land in which they died, thus honouring the battlefield. However, Margaret Thatcher bowed to public opinion and allowed the families of the fallen men the option of having the remains of their loved ones repatriated. In all, seventeen were buried on the island, three at other sites. Others were buried at sea. The landing ship, RFA *Sir Bedivere*, brought 64 bodies back to Britain for burial. For Sara Jones this was not an option. She respected the tradition that 'H' must lie where he fell.

On 4 November Mrs Jones and her two sons, David and Rupert, attended the investiture at Buckingham Palace. Both boys later followed their father into the Devon and Dorset Regiment.

Colonel 'H' Jones is commemorated by a trophy at the annual Bisley inter-country shooting competition, a memorial at Eton College and a plaque on a tree on a coastal footpath near his home village of Kingswear in South Devon. In Aldershot, there is an 'H' Jones Crescent and Lowestoft has a pub called The Colonel H. His portrait hangs in the officers' mess of the Devon and Dorsets, and the School of Infantry in Warminster. His Victoria Cross is kept at the National Army Museum in London, while, out on the Falklands, the islanders built a small cairn of white stones on the spot where he was killed.

CHAPTER TEN

'BRAVEST OF
THE BRAVE'

SERGEANT IAN MCKAY

12 June, 3rd Battalion, Parachute Regiment (Posthumous)

Ian McKay could have been a soccer player if he had not been a soldier. At the time he enlisted he was training with Sheffield United Football Club and turned down an offer from Doncaster Rovers. A keen sportsman at school, he also won junior awards and titles in local championships in badminton, tennis, cricket and athletics.

Born on 7 May 1953 in Sheffield, he was educated at Blackburn primary school, Roughwood Infant and Junior School and Rotherham Grammar School. His father, a steelworker, was not keen on the army and would have preferred that his son train as a physical-education teacher. But Ian had his heart set on joining the Parachute Regiment. He told his father that, if he would not give his consent to his enlisting when he was seventeen, he would wait until he was eighteen and enlist then when he did not need his parents' permission.

Ian McKay had also done well academically at school, collecting six O-levels. It was suggested that he stay on to get his A-levels, then try to get into the Royal Military Academy, Sandhurst. But he was impatient to get on with soldiering and work his way up through the ranks. Three months after his seventeenth birthday, he joined up. Six months later, he was a qualified paratrooper and was posted to the 1st Battalion of the Parachute Regiment – 1 Para.

In March 1971, while he was still only seventeen, he was sent to Northern Ireland. Soon after he arrived, three young Scottish soldiers, all under eighteen, were killed in a single incident. The victims' youth caused public disquiet. McKay was posted back to England to await his birthday. This was ironic, because three seventeen-year-olds fought and died alongside Ian McKay on Mount Longdon. One was killed on his eighteenth birthday, while another, Private Jason Burt, was shot dead in the action that earned McKay his VC.

Once McKay's eighteenth birthday passed, he returned to Northern Ireland and was there in time for 'Bloody Sunday'. On 30 January 1972, the Northern Ireland Civil Rights Association organised a peaceful, but illegal, demonstration in Londonderry against the UK government's policy of internment without trial. Around ten thousand people turned out. McKay was with a support company of 1 Para, sent to back up the police, who were trying to prevent the march reaching the city centre. While the main body of the march headed off towards Free Derry Corner, some of the demonstrators confronted the soldiers. Stones and other projectiles were thrown. The troops responded by firing rubber bullets and with a water cannon.

Although in reserve, since they were nearing the end of their eighteen-month tour of the province, 1 Para were the most experienced unit on hand. The brigade commander sent them in to arrest the ringleaders. Who fired the first shot still remains open to question. The Paras insist that they fired back only after they were fired on. Demonstrators contended that military snipers opened fire on the unarmed protesters.

When the support company left their vehicles in Rossville Street, McKay said, they were fired on from the nearby Rossville Flats. He was with a mortar platoon and heard a burst of fire from a semi-automatic rifle a few minutes after hitting the street. The crowd were throwing stones, bricks and petrol and acid bombs. An acid bomb landed near McKay, splashing his leg. He thought he saw the man who had thrown it on the third floor of the flats. He yelled to his sergeant, who gave him permission to shoot. McKay loosed off two quick shots, but thought he missed. Nevertheless, by the end of the day, thirteen demonstrators lay dead. Another fourteen were injured; one of whom died of his wounds.

The Prime Minister, Edward Heath, ordered an inquiry under Lord Chief Justice Widgery. McKay appeared as Private 'T' to protect his identity. Widgery concluded that, while none of those who had died carried weapons, the demonstrators had fired the first shot. But the local Londonderry coroner maintained that the deaths of the protesters was 'unadulterated murder'. In the outcry that followed, McKay and the other soldiers who had given evidence were excused further service in Northern Ireland. In 1998, Prime Minister Tony Blair set up a fresh inquiry under Lord Saville. This again confirmed that none of the dead were armed.

Over the next ten years, McKay worked his way up to the rank of sergeant. He got married and had two children. His family described him as 'a quite, introverted character'. But there was a determined streak in him, perhaps a Yorkshire cussedness. He did not like to lose. His commanding officer on the Falklands described him as bright, cheerful, enthusiastic, outgoing, interesting and utterly dedicated to his profession.

By the time the Falklands War broke out, McKay was an instructor at Aldershot, where he trained recruits. Had he not been killed, it is thought that he would have been to Sandhurst as a senior NCO instructor of officer cadets. This was an elite posting and often a stepping stone to higher ranks.

Shortly before setting sail on the *Canberra* to the Falklands via Ascension Island on 9 April, McKay was transferred to 3 Para as platoon sergeant of 4 Platoon, B Company, under Lieutenant Andrew Bickerdike. On board ship McKay spent much of his time getting to know the men in this new platoon. Otherwise, they were kept busy with medical and weapon training, briefings, physical training and sunbathing.

Off the Falklands, 3 Para were transferred to HMS *Intrepid* since it was considered too much of a risk to have the entire brigade together on board *Canberra*. The weather was foul and a hitch in the first wave delayed their landing for almost an hour.

In that time, most of the Paras were seasick in their landing craft, though they were grateful that the bad weather would keep the Argentine air force away.

They were to land at 0930 on Green Beach 1, but a sandbar some 50 yards short of the beach meant that some last-minute improvisation had to be made. McKay's B Company, who were the first to land, got wet. A Company, who were next, had to crossdeck from their landing craft, which had grounded on the obstacle. C Company's landing craft made landfall about half a mile short of the beach, and they had to march to the proper landing site carrying their 50-pound rucksacks and other kit, though their company commander, Major Martin Osbourne, said that a 'half-a-mile tab [walk] to the mortarline' was a fair exchange for a dry landing in the cold but sunny conditions.

B Company secured the beachhead while A Company passed through them and on into Port San Carlos settlement. They knocked on doors and quickly discovered that there were no Argentines in the area. The settlers were wide awake, roused by naval gunfire and the approach of landing craft. They had been expecting the British for days.

Over the next few days, 3 Para cleared Fanning Head above a settlement of Argentine survivors and observation posts. They took with them Tactical Air Control parties. It was not long before Argentine planes began to attack the ships in San Carlos Water. The soldiers and marines already ashore fired back with machine guns and rifles. A 3 Para machine-gun crew claimed to have shot down an Argentine Mirage fighter from its position on Fanning Head.

But 3 Para did not go into action in earnest for three weeks – and then it was on the other side of the island in the hills overlooking the islands' capital, Port Stanley. First they had to get there. The loss of the *Atlantic Conveyor* had left the British short of helicopters. That left 45 Commando and 3 Para with the LPC – the 'Leather Personnel Carrier', in other words, the boot. They would have to walk – or 'tab' as the Paras called it. It was a distance of 50 miles, 40 of which were covered in two exhausting night marches on 27–8 and 29–30 May. The terrain was rough, the weather foul and each man had to carry up to 140 pounds of equipment. If a soldier sat down, he would need assistance to get up again.

As 2 Para set off for their attack on Goose Green, 3 Para set off for Port Stanley. The route they were to take was well marked on the map, but there were no signs on the ground. They had to wade through peat bogs, ford streams, clamber over jagged rocks and scale peaks. Soon the men were widely dispersed.

'I don't know about the assault of Stanley,' said Colour Sergeant Bill Eades, 'it looks to me more bloody like the retreat from Moscow.'

By day they laid up, concealed themselves and tried rest and get dry – an impossible task given the foul weather and the sodden ground underfoot. Fear of air raids made lighting a stove a hazard and they went without hot food or drink.

The orders were for 3 Para to follow 45 Commando, who were to go on a northerly route to liberate Douglas Station and Teal Inlet along the way. But there was intense rivalry between those who wore the maroon beret of the Parachute Regiment and the green beret of the Royal Marines. The Paras got permission to turn due east. They overtook 45 Commando and stayed ahead of them all the way to Port Stanley.

By the time they reached Estancia House, where they were to regroup prior to the attack on Mount Longdon, the Paras got news of the victory at Goose Green. Brigadier Thompson himself flew over to Estancia House to stop 3 Para there, as their determined forced march had put them way ahead of their supplies and dangerously close to the Argentines' main defences in the hills around Port Stanley.

From Estancia House, Ian McKay wrote home to his parents,

I have never known a more black, windswept and wet place in my life. We spend our life with wet feet, trying to dry out and keep warm. The wind blows constantly, but it is cooling rather than drying. You cannot walk 50 paces anywhere, even on the mountain-sides, without walking in a bog. I thought the Brecon Beacons was bad, but this takes the biscuit.

On the night of 31 May, 3 Para moved onto Mount Estancia and took up defensive positions, ready for the final push into Port Stanley. They could see the western outskirts of the town some 10 miles to the east. The rest of it was obscured by the looming mass of Mount Longdon. It was a fortress, guarded to the south by a minefield and to the east by enemy troops on Wireless Hill. This would leave little room to manoeuvre.

In the meantime, there was a lull. Ian McKay wrote home,

Mind you things are much quieter now than for some time, and finding things to occupy our time is now a problem. Some clown has put our artillery batteries just behind our positions, and as the Argentinian guns try to range in on them they sometimes drop one in around our position... the papers we get mention only the Marines and the Guards, so if we aren't officially here we might as well come home.

In fact, McKay was well aware that after one last push the whole thing would be over. On 9 June he wrote, 'Things should be over one way or another in a week ... we will be home hopefully about two weeks afterwards.'

He was right. But that one last push was to take his life.

With the weather closing in and resupply becoming a problem, they had to move fast. The high ground of Mount Longdon was a key objective of 3 Commando Brigade's plan of advance on Port Stanley. It had a narrow ridge around 1,200 metres long, running from northwest to southeast. Its rocky summit stood 120 metres above the low ground on all sides, giving the defenders clear fields of fire of at least 2,000 metres. There was no cover until you reached the boulder-strewn upper slopes.

The mountain was defended by the complete the 7th Infantry Regiment reinforced by specialist elements and snipers from 501 Company of the Argentine Special Forces and from the Marines – 278 men in all. The Argentine commander on Mount Longdon, Major Carlos Salvadores, had had nearly two months to prepare the defences. His men had laid numerous minefields to the west and south, and they had dug trenches and built sangars and bunkers. Phone lines had been laid to his subunits so that he could direct his 81mm- and 120mm-mortar teams, as well as the artillery in the Port Stanley area. There were also numerous machine guns and 105mm recoilless guns and anti-tank missiles in position. And each position had been pre-registered as a defensive fire target, so fire could be directed on them if they were overrun. Major Salvadores also had a radar set that was very successful at picking up the movements of enemy patrols before the main attack, and his snipers had night sights, so they could see the enemy coming even during the hours of darkness. Mount Longdon was the linchpin of the Argentine defences of Port Stanley and they were prepared to fight long and hard to keep it.

On the night of 11 June, having been under bombardment from the Argentine 155mm artillery, 3 Para were ordered to take Mount Longdon. The 45 Commando would seize Two Sisters 2,000 metres (2,188 yards) to the southwest and 42 Commando would take Mount Harriet 2,000 metres to the south of that. If all went well, the units would then push on to Wireless Ridge and Mount Tumbledown – then nothing would lie between them and Port Stanley. So taking Mount Longdon was the beginning of the endgame.

The mountain could be taken only piecemeal, from the west, and the summit was such that only one company could fight along it at a time. Worse, intelligence estimated the enemy strength at a battalion of eight hundred, which they then estimated had been reinforced by another four hundred – giving the defenders a numerical superiority of two to one. Fortunately, they were wildly out. But, as night fell on 11 June, the Paras did not like the odds.

Outflanking the defences was not an option as a large minefield was to the south and known enemy positions were to the east on Wireless Ridge. Reconnaissance patrols had surveyed the hill for nearly two weeks and were fairly certain of the locations of the antipersonnel mines. The summit dominated the open ground around it for several thousand metres, increasing the risks of night movements.

Two principal positions defended the mountain. On the east one was called Full Back, which was known to be heavily defended by machine guns and snipers. On the west was Fly Half, which was the enemy command post and well defended. The northern side of the summit was codenamed Wing Forward and the start line for the attack, which also served as a report line, was called Free Kick. This was located on the forward edge of the forming-up point, on the far bank of a stream that runs south to north into the Murrel River.

For 3 Para's commanding officer, Lieutenant Colonel Hew Pike, the capture of Mount Longdon posed several problems. First was the 5,000-metre (5,468-yard) approach across open ground to the start line. Then his men would have to climb another 1,000 metres (1,093 yards) up the exposed slopes of the mountain, which were probably mined. They would have to attack at night but, as they neared their objective, there was a jumble of boulders that would break up the advancing formation and make them hard to control.

Pike's plan was to move the advance companies by independent routes using D Company as patrol guides. A Company would take on Full Back. B Company was to attack Fly Half, while C Company was held in reserve. The idea was to pass C Company through and onto Wireless Ridge after Longdon was taken, but that proved impossible, since Tumbledown was not captured that night and it dominated the ridge and the ground before it.

Fire support was provided by HMS *Avenger* and 79 Battery of the Royal Artillery. The Battalion's own machine guns and mortars of the support company would establish two fire bases: one at the 91-metre (300-foot) contour west of the mountain and another at Free Kick. Engineering support would be provided 2 Troop, 9 Parachute Squadron of the Royal Engineers. The sappers also provided defence for the 91-metre contour firebase by manning a .30in Browning machine gun to neutralise a similar weapon operated by the Argentines on Two Sisters to the southwest. But the initial advance was to be silent. There would be no softening-up bombardment prior to the attack.

In the run-up to the attack, B Company had established a patrol base beneath the shoulder of Mount Kent. From there they had sent out fighting patrols to reconnoitre Mount Longdon, which they now knew was their objective. McKay was frequently on these recces. Like the other men, he was exhausted, patrolling at night, living in wet trenches by day.

There were few opportunities for sleep, but Pike arranged for each platoon in turn to spend a night in the comparative comfort of the sheep-shearing shed at Estancia House. One night it was 4 Platoon's turn. McKay and Bickerdike were in their sleeping bags when an air-raid warning was sounded. The drill was for everyone to take cover in trenches or under the banks of the nearby inlet. The quartermaster woke the platoon, but neither Bickerdike nor McKay appeared. After five minutes, the QM went and physically dragged out the platoon commander and his sergeant, forcing the platoon to take shelter.

The next morning Bickerdike and McKay were given a bollocking. They had felt that a few hours' undisturbed rest was worth the risk of being hit in an air raid. However, had they been hit, the unnecessary casualties caused might have put the whole operation at risk.

On the night of the 11th, the two assault companies set off with guides from D Company. B Company moved off with 4 Platoon in the lead. The attack began at about 2100 hours and the approach required a four-hour-long night infiltration march under a good moon. B Company commander Major Mike Argue altered his approach when one of the fire support groups cut the B Company column with the result that part of 5 Platoon and 6 Platoon lost contact with the rest for about thirty minutes. Having lost time, Major Argue decided to approach the objective directly, travelling well south of the original route and well to the right of A Company.

The moonlight encouraged the platoons to move closer to the rocks for better cover. Three rifle platoons were formed up with the Company HQ slightly to the left and rear. Six Platoon was on the right, attacking from the southwest of the feature; 4 and 5 Platoons were to the west and northwest with 4 Platoon on the left. As they moved into position, McKay saw the Regimental Aid Post Colour Sergeant Faulkner staggering along carrying a rifle, a machine gun, three hundred rounds of ammunition, missiles and a medical kit. They were firm friends.

'See you in Port Stanley,' said McKay grinning. Within four hours he would be dead.

Despite a solitary star shell, 3 Para had reached the start line without being discovered. They had been lucky. The Argentines had turned off their radar, fearing that the British would detect the signal and use it to shell their positions.

Once B Company reached the rocky ground, they fixed bayonets. Five Platoon fanned out and upwards into improved cover but 4 Platoon were still 640 metres (700 yards) away from the first Argentine trenches and on low ground. At this point, Corporal Milne, who was leading the left forward section of 4 Platoon, stepped on an anti-personnel mine and received serious leg injuries. It also lost the Paras the element of surprise. The Argentines responded with mortar, artillery and machine-gun fire, which fortunately was somewhat inaccurate. 5 Platoon was in good cover behind the rocks and 4 Platoon raced forward through the minefield to close on the enemy. 6 Platoon made contact at the same time, having occupied Fly Half without a fight. Although they had grenaded a number of bunkers on their way through, in the dark they missed one and the enemy within opened fire on the platoon's rear, killing some men before they were silenced.

British support artillery, including naval gunfire, opened up. This added to the noise of machine guns, mortars and rocket launchers.

Having advanced through Fly Half, 6 Platoon had suffered eight casualties, four of them fatal. The platoon commander asked to be allowed to pause to reorganise and treat the wounded. This was granted, though he was advised that he might have to move forward at any moment to give 4 and 5 Platoons fire support. 4 Platoon had moved up on the left, though one of its sections had become intermingled with 5 Platoon, which came under heavy fire from Argentine machine guns as they advanced up the hill. A machine-gun team was pushed further up the rock face to fire into the enemy positions, while the Argentine machine gun was taken out with anti-tank rockets.

Enemy fire now came from the 0.50in Browning further east and was dealt with by a section attack. The gun group gave covering fire as Privates Gough and Grey charged forward and grenaded the position.

The two platoons then fought their way into an area forward of the summit of Fly Half, where the rock ridges started to break up and the ground began to slope away to the east. From there, Full Back could be seen in the distance. Immediately, both platoons came under fire from a well-sited platoon position with a 105mm recoilless gun, a .50in Browning and at least two 7.62mm machine guns. The Argentines also had a number of snipers equipped with night sights and, coming over the ridge, B Company made easy targets. The men of 4 and 5 Platoons were falling fast.

Lieutenant Bickerdike decided to carry out a quick recce of the enemy positions. Taking Sergeant McKay and a few others with him, he edged forward to have a look. He was spotted almost immediately. His signaller was hit in the mouth and Bickerdike was wounded in the thigh.

'Sergeant McKay,' he yelled. 'It's your platoon now.'

McKay could have stayed in the rocks. But he knew that the .50in Browning just 32 metres (35 yards) away was holding them up, although their exact position was hard to pinpoint. McKay grabbed seventeen-year-old Private Burt, Corporal Bailey from 5 Platoon and two other privates. Then he arranged covering fire from three machine-gun teams nearby. When they started firing, McKay leaped up and shouted, 'Let's go.'

The five men rushed the .50in Browning which was build into a substantial sangar and protected by at least a section of riflemen, firing from well-sited trenches. Two of McKay's men fell dead immediately. One of them was Private Burt. The other private took cover, along with McKay and Bailey. But the two NCOs were not done yet. They charged forward again, grenading the first position in the rocks. Then Bailey felt a blow to the hip that felled him. He had been hit by a rifle bullet at a range of 3 metres (10 feet). Undaunted, McKay continued alone.

'The last I saw of him, he was just going on, running towards the remaining positions in that group.'

Unable to move, Bailey heard shouts. Moments later, he was hit again in the neck and hand.

What happened next will never be known. McKay's body was found within a few metres of the bunker with several dead Argentinians nearby. Although McKay's final attack on the machine-gun post had not been an immediate success, it opened the way for a final assault that would take 3 Para all the way to the summit, which was taken by what remained of 4 and 5 Platoons at dawn. B Company's casualties had been 33 per cent. They then pulled back for a final bombardment, before A Company cleared the rest of the hill.

Later, McKay's body was recovered by Sergeant Major Weeks of B Company. He removed the wedding ring, as is customary, and one of the dog tags, then slipped the corpse into a body bag. Weeks was in tears when he and the sergeant major of A Company carried McKay's body down the mountain.

The capture of Mount Longdon cost 3 Para twenty dead and more than forty wounded. B Company alone had lost thirteen dead and twenty-seven wounded, out of 118 who had crossed the start line. The Argentinians had lost fifty dead and 100–150 wounded.

On 11 October 1982, Sergeant Ian McKay was awarded a posthumous Victoria Cross for his bravery. The citation read:

During the night of 11–12 June 1982, 3rd Battalion The Parachute Regiment mounted a silent night attack on an enemy battalion position on Mount Longdon, an important objective in the battle for Port Stanley in the Falkland Islands. Sergeant McKay was platoon sergeant of 4 Platoon, B Company, which after the initial objective had been secured, was ordered to clear the northern side of the long east–west ridge feature, held by the enemy in depth, with strong mutually supporting positions.

By now the enemy were fully alert, and resisting fiercely. As 4 Platoon's advance continued it came under increasingly heavy fire from a number of well-sited enemy machine gun positions on the ridge, and received casualties. Realising that no further advance was possible, the platoon commander ordered the platoon to move from its exposed position to seek shelter among the rocks of the ridge itself. Here it met up with part of 5 Platoon.

The enemy fire was still both heavy and accurate, and the position of the platoons was becoming increasingly hazardous. Taking Sergeant McKay, a corporal and a few others, and covered by supporting machine gun fire, the platoon commander moved forward to reconnoitre the enemy positions but was hit by a bullet in the leg, and command devolved upon Sergeant McKay.

It was clear that instant action was needed if the advance was not to falter and increasing casualties to ensue. Sergeant McKay decided to convert this reconnaissance into an attack in order to eliminate the enemy positions. He was in no doubt of the strength and deployment of the enemy as he undertook this attack. He issued orders, and taking three men with him, broke cover and charged the enemy position.

The assault was met by a hail of fire. The corporal was seriously wounded, a private killed and another wounded. Despite these losses, Sergeant McKay, with complete disregard for his own safety, continued to charge the enemy position alone. On reaching it he dispatched the enemy with grenades, thereby relieving the position of beleaguered 4 and 5 Platoons, who were now able to re-deploy with relative safety. Sergeant McKay, however, was killed at the moment of victory, his body falling on the bunker.

Without doubt Sergeant McKay's action retrieved a most dangerous situation and was instrumental in ensuring the success of the attack. His was a coolly calculated act, the dangers of which must have been only too apparent to him beforehand. Undeterred, he performed with outstanding selflessness, perseverance and courage. With a complete disregard for his own safety, he displayed courage and leadership of the highest order, and was an inspiration to all those around him.

The day after the award was gazetted, Ian McKay's mother received a letter from the mother of another paratrooper, one who had survived the battle for Mount Longdon, expressing her condolences of the loss of her son. It read:

I personally never met him, although my son, Simon, who is 18 years old, was in his platoon during the campaign in the Falklands. Since my son's return to England at the beginning of July he has spoken of Sergeant McKay, and his deep admiration of your son's actions during that time. In fact, had it not been for his bravery I doubt very much that my son would have been returned safely to me.

I know that in the short time that Ian was Simon's platoon sergeant he taught him everything about soldiering, and that he had the utmost respect for your son's dedication.

My son was privileged to have known him, and to

have fought alongside him. He was an inspiration, not only to my son, but I am sure to many others in 3 Para to whom he will be remembered as a great hero in time of conflict.

Ian McKay's widow Marcia received her husband's VC at Buckingham Palace on 9 November 1982. Their five-year-old daughter Melanie was photographed with the medal pinned to her black velvet dress. McKay's father Ken said, 'I'm the proudest man in the world, but I would rather have Ian alive.'

Ian McKay was just 29 years old when he died. His was one of the 64 bodies to be brought back from the Falklands on the *Sir Bedivere*, to be greeted at Marchwood Military Port by a lone piper. He was buried with full military honours at the Aldershot Military Cemetery with fifteen other comrades, including seventeen-year-old Private Burt, on 26 November 1982. The last two men to see him alive helped carry his coffin. They were Corporal Ian Bailey, who was shot and injured four minutes before Ian died, and Colour Sergeant Brian Faulkner, who said, 'Mac was the bravest of the brave.'

Ian McKay's old school, Rotherham Grammar, unveiled a plaque in his honour and in June 1988 Princess Margaret opened the McKay Memorial Cottages in Barnsley (also in South Yorkshire). A portrait of him hangs in Rotherham Town Hall. There is another one in 3 Para's sergeants' mess and a painting of him winning the VC in the officers' mess. Three Para's band play the 'Ian McKay VC' commemorative march and a statuette of him, with a grenade in one hand, a rifle in the other, is presented annually to the winner of an interplatoon competition designed to test marching, shooting and other individual battle skills.

Marcia McKay later presented her husband's medals to the Parachute Regiment, who put them on display in the Imperial War Museum. In 2000, she sold them and they are now in one of the biggest private collections of VCs.

PART V
IRAQ

In August 1990, Iraq invaded neighbouring Kuwait. Iraq's leader Saddam Hussein refused to comply with a United Nations Security Council resolution to withdraw. As the invasion posed a threat to Saudi Arabia, the world's largest oil exporter, the United States, its NATO allies, Egypt, Syria and other Arab nations put together a coalition. They began a military build-up of forces, including 700,000 men, known as Operation Desert Shield.

The UN Security Council then authorised the use of force against Iraq if it did not withdraw from Kuwait by 15 January 1991. On the night of 16–17 January, a massive air attack called Operation Desert Storm started. An immense ground offensive called Operation Desert Sabre followed. Iraqi resistance quickly crumbled. The elite Republican Guard was destroyed after trying to make a stand south of Basra in southeast Iraq, and the retreat of the Iraqi Army became a turkey shoot.

On 28 February 1991, US President George Bush Sr declared a ceasefire. The hope was that internal opposition would rise up and depose Saddam Hussein. It didn't, and Saddam was more or less free to restore his repressive grip on power. The peace terms laid down by the UN were that Iraq was to recognise Kuwait's sovereignty, rid itself of all missiles with a range greater than 145 kilometres (90 miles) and divest itself of weapons of mass destruction – nuclear, chemical and biological. Pending complete compliance, economic sanctions were imposed and the US and Britain maintained no-fly zones.

Frequent interference with the weapons inspectors who were supposed to check on the Iraq disarmament programme led President Bill Clinton to order the bombing of Iraqi military installations. It did no good. Saddam Hussein refused to comply with a renewed UN Security Council resolution – number 1441 – demanding that he re-admit weapons inspectors. In early 2003, US President George W Bush and British Prime Minister Tony Blair insisted that Saddam Hussein was dragging his feet on inspections because he retained proscribed weapons of mass destruction. Other world leaders said that Iraq should be given more time to comply.

On 20 March, the US and Britain began new airstrikes. Then British and American forces invaded. US Special Forces moved in to support the Kurds in the north. The main American force hit central Iraq, taking the capital Baghdad, while the British took Basra and the south. By the middle of April all organised resistance was over. On 13 December Saddam Hussein was captured and handed over to the Iraqi authorities. He went on trial in June 2004. On 5 November 2006, he was found guilty of crimes against humanity and was hanged on 30 December 2006.

However, the downfall of Saddam left a political vacuum. Although a democratically elected government was installed, the country became increasingly lawless. British soldiers found themselves fighting guerrillas made up of former supporters of Saddam Hussein, foreign insurgents and other disaffected elements. At the time of writing, there seems to be no end to the casualties among the coalition forces, insurgents and civilians. So far, only one VC has been awarded in Iraq, though British troop withdrawals have begun.

CHAPTER ELEVEN

LUCKY BLOODY BEHARRY

PRIVATE JOHNSON BEHARRY
1 May and 11 June 2004, 1st Battalion, Princess of Wales's Royal
Regiment

Private Johnson Beharry VC is the first person in nearly forty years to be awarded Britain's highest award for gallantry while still alive. This came as a surprise to his comrades, many of whom thought that, due to developments in modern warfare and the ever-stricter criteria that had to be met before the award was made, the VC would never be won again. Others thought that, after 'H' Jones and Ian McKay on the Falklands, it would be impossible to win the VC and survive. Johnson Beharry proved them wrong on both counts. Perhaps that's why they called him 'Lucky Bloody Beharry'.

Born in Diego Piece, Grenada, on 26 July 1979, he was just

24 when he won the VC. The fourth of a family of eight, he spent a childhood in the Caribbean that was marked by poverty. His father, a brick maker, was a violent alcoholic who eked out an existence tending a neighbour's cow because he could not afford his own. With no money for bottled gas, the family had to forage for wood for the stove in order to cook. Their situation became so desperate that the children were split up among relatives. As a small boy, Johnson had to fetch the water, feed the animals and sweep the hut before walking nearly 5 kilometres (3 miles), barefoot, to school. But he would rather work on cars, or help in the school kitchen, than study. Ever innovative, he made his sick mother a bed from old fruit crates.

He left school at the age of thirteen with no qualifications and did a series of odd jobs, but soon began drinking and taking drugs with other layabout 'limers' in the village. Fearing that he was going the way of his father, his grandmother advised him to leave the island. He taught himself mechanics and eventually raised enough money from painting and decorating to pay his fare to England.

In 1999, he arrived in Hounslow, west London, where he was to live with his father's sister Irene, who treated him like a son. He intended to go to college, but began working as a builder. Making good money on building sites, he fell in again with dope-smoking idlers and spent most of it on beer, rum and marijuana. Looking back, he says, 'I was getting nothing from it. I asked myself why.'

After seeing an army recruitment poster on a train he figured that was a way forward and decided to enlist. The recruiting officer was not impressed with his dreadlocks and cannabis-leaf earrings. He was told to go away and clean up. After six months, he returned without the locks – which were ceremonially shorn at a family dinner party – and they took him.

After training at Catterick, Beharry joined the Princess of Wales's Royal Regiment in August 2001 and became a driver of Warrior armoured vehicles in C Company of the 1st Battalion. His early days in the army were not trouble-free because he was not a conformist. If he was unfairly bullied by an officer, he would object. On cleaning duty, he refused to pick up cigarette butts because he wasn't a smoker. Even later, when on operations, he wore his aunt's silver crucifix round his neck with his dog-tag as a kind of talisman, even though it was against the rules. He seems to have got away with a good deal of minor insubordination because of his driving and mechanical skills – and the imminence of the Iraq war. He was also dedicated to his job. After every patrol, he would stay on, servicing and fussing over his Warrior in the compound, while others disappeared for a shower.

'It's a tank, mate,' they'd say, 'not a bloody woman.'

After three months' service in Kosovo and three months in Northern Ireland – the worst place he had been, he said – he was posted to Iraq in April 2004. Beharry was keen to get to a place where there was real danger – not for danger's sake, but so that he would be kept on his toes in a dangerous place. He was not disappointed. Within fifteen minutes of his being deployed to active duty, the compound he was assigned to came under rocket fire.

On 1 May 2004, he was at the British Army base at Abu Naji, just south of the Iraqi city of Al Amarah. A hundred and sixty kilometres (100 miles) north of Basra, it was a centre of activity of the Iranian-backed Mahdi Army loyal to Muqtada al-Sadr. Just after lunch that day, he was with one of the five 30-tonne Warrior armoured vehicles of 8 Platoon that were lined up facing the gate, ready to go. He was driving Whisky Two Zero, the platoon commander's vehicle, which always leads the patrols.

It was a hot afternoon and Beharry and his best friend, Jamaican-born Troy 'Sammy' Samuels, Whisky Two Zero's gunner, headed for the Quick Response Force Room, a small brick building close to where the Warriors are parked. It was 47°C and they were hoping to catch a precious few minutes' sleep in the shade before being summoned to deploy. But the place was crowded and there was no chance to get settled. Just then, Woody, another of Whisky Two Zero's crew, came to the door and said, 'Looks like party time.'

Another armoured patrol had come under fire from RPGs – rocket-propelled grenades – and 8 Platoon were going to their rescue. Beharry and Sammy picked up their helmets and body armour and headed out of the door. By the time they got outside, the platoon commander, Second Lieutenant Richard Deane, was already lowering himself into the commander's hatch of Whisky Two Zero. Beharry pulled on his body armour, leaped up on the hull and slid into his seat. Once his helmet was on, he ran a quick intercom check.

'Boss, Sammy, can you hear me?'

'Roger,' said Lieutenant Deane.

'Loud and clear,' said Sammy.

He checked that his SA80 combat rifle was in the footwell next to his knee, then pressed the starter button. Once the diesel engine roared into life, he put the vehicle into drive and moved out of the compound.

The road in Al Amarah was rough. The water main was broken and water bubbled up through the asphalt. Beharry drove with the hatch open, otherwise his vision would be badly restricted. But the sewers were broken, too, and the smell of excrement in the hot sun made him gag. Behind him, he heard Lieutenant Deane open his hatch, too.

The street was busy. A man selling watermelons from a cart at the side of the road waved. A motorcycle overtook them. The man on the pillion had an AK-47 slung over his shoulder. Youths on the street corners also brandished AKs. Beharry checked in the mirror that the other four Warriors were following in convoy. Whisky Two Two was 50 metres (55 yards) behind. The rest were spaced out evenly behind him. Whisky Two Two's turret was traversing from right to left, with the gun angled towards the rooftops. Apart from Deane and Beharry, everybody else had his hatch closed.

At the junction ahead, Beharry slowed.

'Bee, what is it?' Lieutenant Deane asked. 'Why are you slowing?'

Beharry said that he felt that something was not right. The junction was clear of people. When he checked in his mirror again, he saw that the road behind them was empty of other traffic. Just a few minutes before, it had been busy. The Warriors were now bunched up and vulnerable. The street was narrow and the houses either side were high. The soldiers nervously looked around them, expecting an ambush, but saw nothing.

Then Sammy came on the intercom.

'Left-hand side,' he shouted. 'There's a kid across the street. Eleven, maybe twelve years old. He's holding what looks like an RPG.'

Before Beharry got a chance to turn and look, the rocket-propelled grenade hit the Warrior. There was a massive explosion and the vehicle shook violently. Beharry grabbed his auntie's cross around his neck and began to pray.

Looking out of the open hatch, Beharry could see nothing. Al Amarah was still like a ghost town. Still dazed from the explosion, he got on the intercom.

'Boss, what was that?' he said, trying to keep the fear from his voice.

But the headphones were dead. There was not even the crackle of static.

'Boss, what's happened?' he asked again.

He tried to crane his neck around to see Lieutenant Deane, but his view was blocked by the turret. However, he could smell burning and heard a scream. Then his training kicked in. Where there is one RPG, there are likely to be more. He jammed his foot hard down on the accelerator, but before the power kicked in a second explosion knocked the back end of the vehicle a couple of metres (about 6 feet) across the road.

The engine spluttered and Beharry feared it was going to die on him. But the revs picked up and he turned the Warrior towards the open road, determined to make a run for it. He saw a barricade of hastily erected breeze blocks too late. But, before he hit it, there was another explosion, bigger than the last. Beharry felt a pressure wave, filled with noise and heat, tearing past him and out of the open hatch. He braced himself for another explosion, but then he felt a more reassuring movement. The Warrior was slowly forcing her way through the makeshift barricade.

From the back of the vehicle he could hear screaming. Then the bullets came down like hailstones, pinging off the Warrior's hull. Gunmen were shooting at them from the rooftops. Then he heard the Warrior reply. However, it was not the rat-a-tat-a-tat of the chain gun on the turret, but Sammy with his SA80 on single shot.

'Drive, Paki,' Sammy shouted. 'For Christ's sake, drive. There's more of them lining up with RPGs.'

Beharry stamped down on the accelerator, but the engine barely responded.

'Move, Beharry. Move, move, move,' yelled Woody from the back.

He called out to the Boss.

'Stop calling the Boss,' Sammy shouted. 'The Boss is dead. He got hit by the first RPG. He's lying on the floor of the turret. He's a mess.'

As Beharry sped down the street, a man in Arab dress ran out into the road and started firing an AK-47. The bullets ricocheted off the Warrior's front armour. Beharry shouted up at Samuels to use the chain gun. But it was jammed. All Sammy had was Lieutenant Deane's rifle.

The man with the AK-47 was now 50 metres (55 yards) away, firing from the hip. A bullet slammed into Beharry's helmet and his head was thrown back against the hatch. But Beharry drove on and, at the last possible moment, the man with the AK-47 leaped back into an alleyway while the Warrior thundered off down the road.

Further down the street, the houses were decked with the black flag of Islam. Beharry feared that the black flags foretold their deaths. Then, out of the corner of his eyes, he saw a movement in the shadows. A man stepped out, heaved a tube over his shoulder and fired. Beharry should have yelled 'RPG', but was mesmerised by the shell as it headed towards Warrior. Then he suddenly realised that it was coming straight for him. He ducked and pulled down the hatch, before an explosion tore it from his hand. There was a scream behind and Beharry realised that Samuels has been caught by the blast.

Now, with no hatch to protect him, Beharry made off down the road. Checking in his mirror, he could still see the other vehicles. Plainly, they were following because they thought that Lieutenant Deane was alive and in charge. They did not know that Deane was out of action and that, effectively, Private Beharry was now in command of the convoy.

Beharry suddenly realised that the responsibility for getting the muckers out of this mess now fell to him. The Warrior's crew were depending on him. The platoon following were in his hands too. And the situation was not looking good. Whisky Two Zero had already been hit by three RPGs. It couldn't take another. Fortunately, all they were taking then was small-arms fire, though this was little comfort to Beharry, since his hatch had been blown away and there was nothing to protect him.

Then, at the end of the street, Beharry saw another Warrior.

He pulled up alongside and the head of his commanding officer, Major Coote, appeared. Coote touched the top of his head, signalling for Beharry to follow him to a walled compound. But this afforded little safety. As soon as Major Coote's Warrior came to a halt, bullets were ricocheting off it.

As Beharry began to pull himself out of the hatch, four or five rounds hit the front of the Warrior and he dropped back into his seat. He had a choice now. He could jump out, sprint through the bullets and throw himself behind one of the galvanised-steel and polypropylene barriers nearby, where he would be safe, or he could try to help the rest of his injured crewmates.

He pulled himself out of the hatch again, as a bullet whined through the air above his head. Then he rolled onto the turret and a bullet ricocheted off it a foot from his face. Leaning over the hatch, he saw Lieutenant Deane slumped on the floor. There was blood on his seat, along with the shredded remains of his body armour.

Beharry leaned inside the turret and tapped the back of Lieutenant Deane's helmet. Deane did not move. But Samuels, hunched up next to him, did. He was clutching his sides. The explosion had ripped the clothes from his torso and his chest was covered with burns.

'Sammy, man, it's me,' said Beharry.

Samuels looked up. He face was badly burned and his eyes were bloodshot.

'Paki?' he said.

Beharry grabbed Samuels by the waist and tried to pull him

out. But, at that moment, a bullet hit the hatch. Beharry let go and Samuels fell back, prompting a groan from Lieutenant Deane. It was only then that they realised he was alive.

By this time smoke was pouring into the turret from deep inside the vehicle. The heat was building up and it was plain that the vehicle was getting ready to blow up. Beharry and Samuels tried to pull Deane out, while bullets pinged from the armour all around them.

Despite the constant fire, they manage to manoeuvre Lieutenant Deane out of the hatch. Beharry slung him over his shoulders and carried him to Major Coote's Warrior. Once he was safely inside, Beharry went back to get Samuels.

Sammy was already halfway out of the hatch. His face was covered with so much blood that Beharry was not sure that he could see. The sniper opened up again and Beharry grabbed Samuels and pulled him down behind the turret. They slid down the Warrior's hull. Once they were down on the ground, Beharry dragged Samuels over to Coote's Warrior, then went back to Whisky Two Zero. Smoke was now pouring from the turret. He ran around to the back and opened the door – to be confronted by Big Erv, the radio operator, who was pointing his SA80 at Beharry's chest. His face was cover in blood and there was wild look in his eyes. At any minute, Beharry thought, he might pull the trigger.

'Erv, it's Beharry!' said Woody, appearing through the smoke behind him. Erv lowered his rifle.

Woody's face was covered in cuts. His helmet had been blown off and he had lost most of his hair. There was blood on the floor and the walls, and there was a hole through the hull where an RPG had hit.

A sergeant came running up and told them to get out. The vehicle was on fire. Together they got Big Erv and Woody to safety. The sixth crew man, Clifton, though wounded by shrapnel, was safe.

Once he knew that all his crewmates had been taken care of, Beharry asked Major Coote what they should do next.

'Follow me,' shouted the major through the noise of gunfire. 'We're going to drive out of the contact area.'

Beharry was halfway back to Whisky Two Zero when he realised that he had not told Major Coote how badly damaged the Warrior was. But it was too late. He could already hear Coote's Warrior moving off. Whisky Two Zero's engine was still running and he managed to follow Coote a little way. Then the major realised that he was in trouble and stopped. He told Beharry to take the Warrior back to the walled compound. He was fired on most of the way, but when he got there he saw the other Warriors from 8 Platoon and realised that, if he parked there and Whisky Two Zero blew up, she would take them with her. So he risked his life again to manoeuvre the Warrior behind a blast wall. Then he switched off the engine and pulled the handle that discharged the built-in fire extinguisher, which disabled the vehicle.

He grabbed his rifle and clambered out of the vehicle, then climbed up onto the turret to disable the main armaments. The last thing his platoon needed was the Mahdi army turning the Warrior's weapons on them. He grabbed Lieutenant Deane's rifle and his own, Deane's and Samuel's rucksacks and ran back to Coote's Warrior. Once in the back, he collapsed.

When Beharry came round, he was in hospital. He asked the doctor about the rest of the crew. They had all survived. Beharry himself was suffering from heat exhaustion, but later his sergeant major showed him his helmet. It had a hole in the top of it where it had been hit by a bullet from an AK-47. He was lucky to be alive.

After spending a night in an army medical centre, Beharry was returned to active duty on 3 May, driving a replacement Whisky Two Zero. It was once again to be commanded by Lieutenant Deane who, after recovering from shrapnel wounds, returned to active duty a week later. On the night of 11 June 2004, they were called out as part of a rapid-reaction force tasked with cutting off a mortar team that had attacked the coalition forces in Al Amarah. Moving through the dark streets at night, they drove straight into another ambush.

Beharry spotted a flash to his left. Lieutenant Deane shouted a warning. Samuels called out his name. Then he saw the RPG with its fins flipped out, followed by a plume of smoke, less than the length of a vehicle away. It hit the frontal armour just 15 centimetres (6 inches) above Beharry's head. For a moment he was stunned. Then Lieutenant Deane's persistent calling got through to him.

'Bee, can you hear me?' he asked

'I hear you,' said Beharry, still groggy.

'Get us out of here!' yelled the lieutenant. 'Go, go, go!'

Barely conscious of where he was, Beharry slipped the Warrior into reverse and hit the accelerator. It shot backwards.

'Go, Paki, go!' yelled Samuels. 'There's more of 'em out there. They're lining up for another shot!'

More RPGs pounded into Whisky Two Zero, incapacitating Lieutenant Deane and wounding several of the crew. Nevertheless, despite his extensive injuries, Beharry held firm. The Warrior raced backwards across 200 metres (218 yards) of open ground. Then through the darkness they saw another Warrior.

'Follow him, Bee,' said Deane.

'OK,' said Beharry. But he could not move his foot. He could drive no further. However, at least they were out of the immediate danger zone. Beharry was still conscious when Sergeant Chris Broome (a.k.a. 'Broomstick') from the other Warrior opened the hatch and pulled him out.

'Stick, am I dying?' asked Beharry.

'Nah, mate, you're not dying,' said Broome.

However, he had such severe head wounds that doctors feared he would not survive. Extensive brain surgery was needed. His skull had been smashed like an eggshell and had to be reconstructed. After weeks in a coma, Beharry woke to find himself back in Britain. His cousin, Gavin, was at his bedside, telling him that the newspapers were saying he should be given the Victoria Cross.

'I didn't do nothing, Gav,' Beharry said. 'I was just doing me duty. Any of me mates would've done the same.'

But the papers said that, by his action alone, he saved the lives of thirty other men. He was a hero.

'I don't feel like a hero,' said Beharry. 'I feel like a Kentucky Fried Chicken and I want to get out of here.'

A few days later, Gavin smuggled him out to the local KFC. Waiting in the queue, a girl asked Beharry what had happened.

'I got shot in the head,' he said.

Earlier, he had caught sight of himself in a bathroom mirror and was shocked to see that his head was twice its normal size. There were deep bruises around his eyes. His pupils were almost hidden by swollen lids and there was a line of staples where his face met his scalp. But he figured that, with a bandage around his head, and the jeans, T-shirt and trainers his cousin had bought, no one would notice.

He was awarded the VC on 18 March 2005.

'When I first heard the news, I didn't know what VC meant,' Beharry said. 'Now I realise how big it is, I can't see what I've done to deserve it. I was just doing what I was trained to do. I didn't do it for a medal, I didn't do it for any other reason than I was in a position where I could help, and I helped. I was hoping I could save my colleagues, and I did. That's the great part about it, and that's what the medal represents.'

But there was rather more to it than that. The citation reads:

Private Beharry carried out two individual acts of great heroism by which he saved the lives of his comrades. Both were in direct face of the enemy, under intense fire, at great personal risk to himself (one leading to his sustaining very serious injuries). His valour is worthy of the highest recognition.

In the early hours of 1 May 2004 Beharry's company was ordered to replenish an isolated Coalition Forces outpost located in the centre of the troubled city of Al Amarah. He was the driver of a platoon commander's Warrior armoured fighting vehicle. His platoon was the company's reserve force and was placed on immediate notice to move. As the main elements of his company were moving into the city to carry out the replenishment, they were re-tasked to fight through a series of enemy ambushes in order to extract a foot patrol that had become pinned down under sustained small arms and heavy machine gun fire and improvised explosive device and rocket-propelled grenade attack.

Beharry's platoon was tasked over the radio to come to the assistance of the remainder of the company, who were attempting to extract the isolated foot patrol. As his platoon passed a roundabout, en route to the pinned-down patrol, they became aware that the road to the front was empty of all civilians and traffic – an indicator of a potential ambush ahead. The platoon commander ordered the vehicle to halt, so that he could assess the situation. The vehicle was then immediately hit by multiple rocket-propelled grenades. Eyewitnesses report that the vehicle was engulfed in a number of violent explosions, which physically rocked the 30-tonne Warrior.

As a result of this ferocious initial volley of fire, both the platoon commander and the vehicle's gunner were incapacitated by concussion and other wounds, and a number of the soldiers in the rear of the vehicle were also wounded. Due to damage sustained in the blast to the vehicle's radio systems, Beharry had no means of communication with either his turret crew or any of the other Warrior vehicles deployed around him. He did not know if his commander or crewmen were still alive, or how serious their injuries may be. In this confusing and dangerous situation, on his own initiative, he closed his driver's hatch and moved forward through the ambush position to try to establish some form of communications, halting just short of a barricade placed across the road.

The vehicle was hit again by sustained rocket-propelled grenade attack from insurgent fighters in the alleyways and on rooftops around his vehicle. Further damage to the Warrior from these explosions caused it to catch fire and fill rapidly with thick, noxious smoke. Beharry opened up his armoured hatch cover to clear his view and orientate himself to the situation. He still had no radio communications and was now acting on his own initiative, as the lead vehicle of a six-Warrior convoy in an enemy-controlled area of the city at night. He assessed that his best course of action to save the lives of his crew was to push through, out of the ambush. He drove his Warrior directly through the barricade, not knowing if there were mines or improvised explosive devices placed there to destroy his vehicle. By doing this he was able to lead the remaining five Warriors behind him towards safety.

As the smoke in his driver's tunnel cleared, he was just able to make out the shape of another rocket-propelled grenade in flight heading directly towards him. He pulled the heavy armoured hatch down with one hand, whilst still controlling his vehicle with the other. However, the overpressure from the explosion of the rocket wrenched the hatch out of his grip, and the flames and force of the blast passed directly over him, down the driver's tunnel, further wounding the semi-conscious gunner in the turret. The impact of this rocket destroyed Beharry's armoured periscope, so he was forced to drive the vehicle through the remainder of the ambushed route, some 1,500 metres [1,650 yards] long, with his hatch opened up and his head exposed to enemy fire, all the time with no communications with any other vehicle. During this long surge through the ambushes the vehicle was again struck by rocket-propelled grenades and small arms fire. While his head remained out of the hatch, to enable him to see the route ahead, he was directly exposed to much of this fire, and was himself hit by a 7.62mm bullet, which penetrated his helmet and remained lodged on its inner surface.

Despite this harrowing weight of incoming fire Beharry continued to push through the extended ambush, still leading his platoon until he broke clean. He then visually identified another Warrior from his company and followed it through the streets of Al Amarah to the outside of the Cimic House outpost, which was receiving small-arms fire from the surrounding area. Once he had brought his vehicle to a halt outside, without thought for his own personal safety, he climbed onto the turret of the still-burning vehicle and, seemingly oblivious to the incoming enemy small-arms fire, manhandled his wounded platoon commander out of the turret, off the vehicle and to the safety of a nearby Warrior. He then returned once again to his vehicle and again mounted the exposed turret to lift out the vehicle's gunner and move him to a position of safety. Exposing himself yet again to enemy fire he returned to the rear of the burning vehicle to lead the disoriented and shocked dismounts and casualties to safety. Remounting his burning vehicle for the third time, he drove it through a complex chicane and into the security of the defended perimeter of the outpost, thus denying it to the enemy. Only at this stage did Beharry pull the fire extinguisher handles, immobilising the engine of the vehicle, dismounted and then moved himself into the relative safety of the back of another Warrior. Once inside, Beharry collapsed from the sheer physical and mental exhaustion of his efforts and was subsequently himself evacuated.

Having returned to duty following medical treatment, on the 11 June 2004 Beharry's Warrior was part of a quick reaction force tasked to attempt to cut off a mortar team that had attacked a Coalition Force base in Al Amarah. As the lead vehicle of the platoon he was moving rapidly through the dark city streets towards the suspected firing point, when his vehicle was ambushed by the enemy from a series of rooftop positions. During this initial heavy weight of enemy fire, a rocket-propelled grenade detonated on the vehicle's frontal armour, just 6 inches [15 centimetres] from Beharry's head, resulting in a serious head injury. Other rockets struck the turret and sides of the vehicle, incapacitating his commander and injuring several of the crew.

With the blood from his head injury obscuring his vision, Beharry managed to continue to control his vehicle, and forcefully reversed the Warrior out of the ambush area. The vehicle continued to move until it struck the wall of a nearby building and came to rest. Beharry then lost consciousness as a result of his wounds. By moving the vehicle out of the enemy's chosen killing area he enabled other Warrior crews to be able to extract his crew from his vehicle, with a greatly reduced risk from incoming fire. Despite receiving a serious head injury, which later saw him being listed as very seriously injured and in a coma for some time, his level-headed actions in the face of heavy and accurate enemy fire at short range again almost certainly saved the lives of his crew and provided the conditions for their safe evacuation to medical treatment.

Beharry displayed repeated extreme gallantry and unquestioned valour, despite intense direct attacks, personal injury and damage to his vehicle in the face of relentless enemy action.

General Sir Mike Jackson, Chief of the General Staff, said, 'It's the most extraordinary story of one man's courage and the way in which he risked his life for his comrades, for his own young officer in particular, not once, but twice. I can't remember when I was last so proud of the army as I am today.'

His commanding officer in Iraq, Lieutenant Colonel Matt Maer, said, 'To do what he did showed extraordinary courage. Hero is a grossly overused term these days, but he is a true hero.'

Grenada's Prime Minister, Dr Keith Mitchell, said, 'Private Beharry's achievement will inspire the young men and women of Grenada, and should be used as a lesson which demonstrates that the most difficult challenges and trying times can be overcome.'

'I was just doing my job and the best for my colleagues,' said Beharry. 'I think someone else would have done the same thing… Maybe I was brave, I don't know. At the time I was just doing the job, I didn't have time for other thoughts.'

He said that he was not afraid while in action, but admitted that he felt a bit scared about what he had done afterwards. Asked what was going through his mind at the time, he replied, 'An RPG.'

Private Troy Samuels was awarded the Military Cross for his actions alongside Private Beharry, and Sergeant Chris Broome, who was wounded in the action, was awarded the Conspicuous Gallantry Cross, which is second only to the VC, for bravery in the face of the enemy.

On 27 April 2005, Johnson Beharry went to Buckingham Palace to receive his VC.

'You're a very special person,' said the Queen as she pinned the medal onto his chest. Then, with masterly understatement, she added, 'It's been rather a long time since I've awarded one of these.'

'It was a great day for me,' Beharry said. 'But, at the end of the ceremony, my shoulder and back were killing me. The pain was so bad, I couldn't wait to get out of that uniform.'

His award brought him a book deal for his autobiography, reputedly worth £1 million, which he used to set up a foundation for underprivileged children in Grenada. But his injuries have left Johnson Beharry debilitated. He is in constant pain and suffers from searing headaches, which, he says, make him feel as if there were ants crawling about inside his brain.

He remained in the army but was not fit enough to go back to the front line and consequently had no real role. He was promoted to lance corporal, but denied any ambition to be Britain's first black general.

'I would like to stay in uniform but, because of my medical problems, I can't tell what the future will bring,' he said. But he is still very much a soldier. 'I still feel like I am one of the lads. We still have a great relationship and if they feel differently towards me they certainly don't show it. My battalion is out in Iraq at the moment and, man, I wish I was out there with them. They return home this month so I just hope everyone comes back safe.'

Beharry's churchgoing wife Lynthia, his childhood sweet-heart, complained that his injuries had made him a changed man and their marriage ended. Once a laid-back kind of guy, he has become a man on a short fuse, and the fear of what might happen if he loses his temper limits his social life.

'I get angry really easy now,' he said. 'Any little thing will trigger me off. Silly little things, but I just take them the wrong way. I used to go clubbing every night. Now I don't want to go out. I just don't have that get-up-and-go any more. I still enjoy life, but I am happier sitting at home than going to a club. I don't want to get myself in trouble, so I prefer to stay away. Since the accident, I see life different. I do a lot of things different.'

His enforced celebrity and enforced idleness changed his life and he was seen out with the sophisticated Grenadian beauty Tamara Vincent. Relatives back home in Grenada sold stories to the newspapers saying that he was puffed up by his award.

'Everyone forgot the old person. They see this great person and they expect me to be that person. It is hard to live to please everyone,' he said. 'People expect so much from me now and it's hard to live up to their expectations. Everyone thinks, because I received the Victoria Cross, I get a wall of money and they expect me to give them whatever they ask for. But the VC is just a medal.

'I don't point a finger at anyone. It's my whole family on my mother's side. They give stories about me to the papers and nothing is true. They don't know me. I was never close to them. I don't think they know what is love. It's not like I want them to bow to me, to worship me. But they treat me like I owe them something. All they think about is themselves and what they can get.'

But family disputes are not the worst of his troubles.

'I think the most difficult part is dealing with my injuries,' he said. 'I still have a lot of pain in my shoulder, back and head and I suffer flashbacks. I just hope that one day it will all go away and never come back.'

Was it worth it? Beharry was asked. Was there was ever a moment when he wished he were an unknown soldier again without his VC?

'I am proud of it,' he replied. 'I didn't do it because I wanted a medal. I did it because these soldiers were in danger and I could help them. I feel good knowing that they are all alive and without injury and knowing that it's me that saved them. I don't think I would have been able to live with myself knowing I could have done something and I didn't. To me the medal represents all those guys who have a life. But you don't get something like this for free. You get it and survive with the pain – or you get it and die.'

PART VI
AFGHANISTAN

From 1979 to 1992, the Islamic mujahedeen fought the armed forces of the Soviet Union, who had entered Afghanistan to prop up the communist government there. Among their ranks were a number of foreign fighters including the Saudi citizen Osama bin Laden, and, as the Cold War was still going on at the time, they were provided with weapons by the US.

Once the Soviets had left, there was a civil war in Afghanistan, which was eventually won by the Taliban, a puritanical Islamic group. Osama bin Laden returned home a hero, but soon became disaffected by the corruption of the Saudi government and his own wealthy family. During the First Gulf War, bin Laden believed that he and his Muslim fighters should defend the holy sites of Islam. He was horrified that the Saudi Arabian government preferred the protection of US troops.

Bin Laden set up a terrorist organisation called al-Qaeda – the Base. Its aim was to fight a jihad or holy war to force the US out of the Gulf. To do so, he organised and funded attacks on US troops in Saudi Arabia and tourists in Egypt, and the bombing of US embassies in Nairobi and Dar es Salaam, killing nearly 300 people. Accused of subversion, he fled to the Sudan. Expelled from there, he returned to Afghanistan, where the Taliban gave him sanctuary.

From the al-Qaeda training camps in Afghanistan, bin Laden planned to take the war to the enemy and organised the 11 September 2001 attacks on the twin towers of the World Trade Center in New York and the Pentagon in Arlington, Virginia.

When the Taliban refused to extradite bin Laden, the US launched Operation Enduring Freedom, with British support, to remove it from power. America and Britain invaded Afghanistan and installed a pro-Western government but, despite extensive searches, bin Laden has not been caught. However, continuing unrest has presented the West few opportunities to rebuilt Afghanistan's war-damaged infrastructure and the country's porous borders have allowed the Taliban to reassert itself.

While the soldiers of other NATO nations were restricted to the relatively peaceful north, British troops were committed to Helmand Province in the south of Afghanistan, where the fighting with the Taliban was the most intense. Casualties continue to mount and, at the time of writing, more British troops are being committed. So far two VCs have been won in Afghanistan - one of them awarded posthumously.

CHAPTER TWELVE

A CONSUMMATE PROFESSIONAL

CORPORAL BRYAN BUDD

27 July and 20 August 2006, 3rd Battalion, the Parachute Regiment
(Posthumous)

There is controversy surrounding the death of Corporal Bryan
Budd VC. It is feared that he was killed by his own comrades,
accidentally, during a ferocious clash with the Taliban in
Helmand Province in August 2006. A comrade speaking for 3
Para in Colchester, Essex, where 29-year-old Corporal Budd was
based, said, 'The horrible truth that is dawning on us is that
Bryan's death was probably caused by friendly fire. Friendly fire
is bad enough at the best of times, but when it claims the life of
a VC hero it is unbelievable.

'Yet our view is that, whatever the circumstances, Bryan fully
deserved his VC and died heroically while fighting to save his

comrades. Obviously, his comrades are extremely cut up after being warned that one of them may have unwittingly fired the fatal shots which killed him.'

Born on 16 July 1977 in Scunthorpe, Lincolnshire, Bryan Budd enlisted into the Parachute Regiment in December 1995 at the age of eighteen. He then passed the rigorous selection process for 16 Air Assault Brigade's Pathfinder Platoon, an elite unit specially trained for long-range reconnaissance missions. In that unit, he served in many operational theatres, including the former Yugoslavia, Sierra Leone, Macedonia, Afghanistan and Iraq.

In May 2002, Budd passed his section commander's battle course with distinction, and was due to be promoted to platoon sergeant. He was also a qualified combat survival instructor, rock climber and free-fall parachutist. He was posted to the Army Foundation College in Harrogate in 2004, where he trained young soldiers.

He and his wife lived in Ripon, Yorkshire. He loved the outdoors and would spend whatever time he could enjoying the countryside.

In June 2006, he joined A Company of 3 Para in Helmand Province, Afghanistan, in the middle of Operation Herrick IV, when the company was principally concerned with helping the Afghan government counter a resurgence in Taliban activity in and around the town of Sangin. Initially deployed to help rebuild the war-torn country, 3 Para found themselves in bloody battles against Taliban insurgents, who launched near-suicidal assaults in large numbers. Daily gunfights were fought as the British force pushed into the lawless northern towns of the province to wrest power from the Taliban and opium warlords.

Softly spoken and generous, Bryan Budd had quickly become a very popular leader.

'All the blokes had huge respect for him,' said a comrade. 'That's not an easy thing to achieve when you're so new to a tight-knit company. He was a quiet guy but he really opened up when you got to know him. He used to tell us how much he loved the army and the Parachute Regiment and was going to serve out his full 22 years.'

On 27 July, Corporal Budd's section were on a patrol when they identified and engaged two enemy gunmen on the roof of a building in the centre of Sangin. Without regard for his own safety, he led an assault where the enemy fire was heaviest. Comrades of Corporal Budd, who was due to be promoted to sergeant, said he single-handedly stormed a building using hand grenades and his rifle to kill the enemy. His gallant action allowed a wounded soldier to be evacuated to safety, where he subsequently received lifesaving treatment.

Corporal Budd was due to go home on 25 August, but on the 20th he was again engaged in heavy fighting near Sangin District Centre. He and his men were ordered to hold a small, isolated coalition outpost – dubbed a platoon house – against a vicious daily onslaught by the Taliban that had been going on for months.

A comrade said, 'We were sent out to protect some engineers who were blowing holes in a compound 500 metres [1,640 yards] away from the platoon house. That was so we could cut through the compound quickly and avoid enemy fire when we were out on patrol. There were three sections of us out, a total of 24 guys, all spread out in a head-high cornfield around the compound. Bryan was the first to spot about four Taliban approaching, really close to us, only about 50 metres [55 yards] away.'

Using only hand signals, Budd led his section in a flanking manoeuvre round to the cornfield's outskirts to try to cut them off. But the section was spotted by the enemy before they could get there, and they opened fire. Then a further contingent of Taliban hidden behind a wall further back also opened up on the section.

'The guys were taking heavy fire from two positions,' said his mate. 'The enemy were just blatting away, their AK-47s above their heads, and rounds were coming in from all over the shop.'

One soldier got a bullet in the shoulder. Another was shot in the nose.

'Everyone was kneeling or lying down, trying to take cover. It was mayhem.'

Bryan Budd could see that his men were in mortal danger and knew that he had to do something about it.

'That's when Bryan made his move. He knew how dangerous it was but he obviously decided it was his responsibility to destroy the threat, because the enemy were cutting us to pieces.'

Bryan Budd got up and rushed straight through the corn in the direction of the Taliban just 20 metres (22 yards) away.

'We heard Bryan's rifle open up on them on fully automatic mode,' said his comrade-in-arms, 'but that was the last anyone heard of him. All contact was lost with Bryan. Straight afterwards, the enemy's fire lessened and allowed the rest of his section to withdraw back to safety so the casualties could be treated.'

Budd was listed missing in action and the whole company were then sent back to try to find him. Lance Corporal Carse, who helped recover his friend's body, said, 'A patrol had been ambushed with machine guns and there was a Para missing. We formed a quick-reaction force and with a Para sniper we went out to find him. We ran out through the gates of the platoon house under fire. We took a lot of fire as we got into a cornfield where the soldier was and then we had to fight our way back to the platoon house with Corporal Budd. He was one of the best and bravest soldiers I had met – he had taken on the Taliban virtually on his own.'

'We went into the cornfield to fight our way forward,' said another comrade. 'Apache and Harrier air support was called in, and after a long fight we beat the Taliban back. About an hour later some of the lads found Bryan's body beside two dead Taliban. It was obvious he was the one who had wasted them but he was obviously hit at the same time – by either them or the fighters behind the wall. He was badly wounded and he had no pulse.'

The company sergeant major rushed forward on a quad bike to collect him and carried him back to the platoon house. But there was nothing anyone could do for him by then and he was declared dead.

'What Bryan did was amazing,' his comrade added. 'He made the ultimate sacrifice for his men.'

There was no doubt among his men that he deserved the VC. His regiment also backed the award.

'Corporal Budd ticks almost every box needed for a VC,' a spokesman for 3 Para said.

The award was finally made on 14 December 2006. The citation reads:

During July and August 2006, A Company, 3rd Battalion, the Parachute Regiment were deployed in the District Centre at Sangin. They were constantly under sustained attack from a combination of Taliban small arms, rocket-propelled grenades, mortar and rocket fire.

On 27 July 2006, whilst on a routine patrol, Corporal Bryan Budd's section identified and engaged two enemy gunmen on the roof of a building in the centre of Sangin. During the ensuing fierce fire-fight, two of Corporal Budd's section were hit. One was seriously injured and collapsed in the open ground, where he remained exposed to enemy fire, with rounds striking the ground around him. Corporal Budd realised that he needed to regain the initiative and that the enemy needed to be driven back so that the casualty could be evacuated.

Under fire, he personally led the attack on the building where the enemy fire was heaviest, forcing the remaining fighters to flee across an open field where they were successfully engaged. This courageous and prompt action proved decisive in breaking the enemy and was undertaken at great personal risk. Corporal Budd's decisive leadership and conspicuous gallantry allowed his wounded colleague to be evacuated to safety where he subsequently received life-saving treatment.

A month later, on 20 August 2006, Corporal Budd was leading his section on the right forward flank of a platoon clearance patrol near Sangin District Centre. Another section was advancing with a Land Rover fitted with a .50 calibre heavy machine gun on the patrol's left flank. Pushing through thick vegetation, Corporal Budd identified a number of enemy fighters 30 metres ahead. Undetected, and in an attempt to surprise and destroy the enemy, Corporal Budd initiated a flanking manoeuvre. However, the enemy spotted the Land Rover on the left flank and the element of surprise was lost for the whole platoon.

In order to regain the initiative, Corporal Budd decided to assault the enemy and ordered his men to follow him. As they moved forward the section came under a withering fire that incapacitated three of his men. The continued enemy fire and these losses forced the section to take cover. But Corporal Budd continued to assault on his own, knowing full well the likely consequences of doing so without the close support of his remaining men. He was wounded but continued to move forward, attacking and killing the enemy as he rushed their position.

Inspired by Corporal Budd's example, the rest of the platoon reorganised and pushed forward their attack, eliminating more of the enemy and eventually forcing their withdrawal. Corporal Budd subsequently died of his wounds, and when his body was later recovered it was found surrounded by three dead Taliban.

Corporal Budd's conspicuous gallantry during these two engagements saved the lives of many of his colleagues. He acted in the full knowledge that the rest of his men had either been struck down or had been forced to go to ground. His determination to press home a single-handed assault against a superior enemy force despite his wounds stands out as a premeditated act of inspirational leadership and supreme valour. In recognition of this, Corporal Budd is awarded the Victoria Cross.

Corporal Bryan Budd's wife, 23-year-old Lorena Budd, herself a serving soldier with the Adjutant General's Corps, was eight months pregnant when her husband died. She later accepted the award at a presentation in the MoD's Main Building.

'I would like to take this opportunity to say how proud I am to be accepting this incredible award on behalf of my husband, Bryan,' she said. 'Bryan, of course, will always be remembered by me as a loving husband and father to our two beautiful daughters, Isabelle and Imogen. This exceptional act of valour, and the subsequent award of the Victoria Cross, is representative of the sort of man Bryan was. He was a proud and passionate Parachute Regiment soldier and he was someone who was prepared to make the very highest sacrifice, doing the job he loved, with his comrades and friends in the regiment he loved.

'Today is a day to remember Bryan, and I take enormous

pride in remembering all his achievements. However, I would now be grateful if me, the girls and our families could be left alone to grieve privately and reflect on our loss at this emotional time. On a final note, I would also like to take this opportunity to thank Major Bruce Radbourne of the Parachute Regiment for all the help he has provided and also for all the support I have received from all of 3 Para.'

She later went to the formal investiture at Buckingham Palace.

'A talented and hardworking soldier, Corporal Budd was the consummate professional,' said a spokesman for the Ministry of Defence, adding,

Universally liked and admired, he was a shining example to those under his command, demonstrating great courage in the face of adversity. He had a keen sense of humour and a natural ability for lightening the mood.

Softly spoken and gracious, he was never hurried or flustered and took everything in his stride. Living in such a beautiful part of the world, he loved the outdoors and would spend whatever time he could there. However, his keenest passion was for his family of which he was incredibly proud. He leaves behind his wife Lorena and daughter Isabelle. The couple were looking forward to the birth of their second child in September.

His commanding officer, Lieutenant Colonel Stuart Tootal, said, 'Corporal Bryan Budd was an outstanding young man who had quickly risen through the ranks in the regiment. Extremely popular, he had a calm and professional manner that inspired confidence in all that worked with him; a natural leader. Bryan died doing the job he loved, leading his men from the front, where he always was. Bryan was proud to call himself a Paratrooper and we were proud to stand beside him. One of the very best in all respects, he will be sadly missed by all his comrades in 3 Para and our thoughts are with his family and friends at this difficult time.'

Later, Lorena was said to have been 'totally devastated' when she learned that her husband's death was probably due to a 'blue-on-blue' incident – that he had accidentally been killed by his own men.

A senior military source said, 'It increasingly looks like this is a terribly tragic case of friendly fire. However, there is no question of taking back Corporal Budd's VC or downgrading it. Even if it is proved conclusively that his death was caused by friendly fire, he fulfilled all the credentials necessary to be awarded the VC. Our deepest sympathies go out to his widow and family who understandably were devastated after being officially informed of this possibility. But the harsh truth is that in close-quarter combat you are almost as likely to be killed by your own side as the enemy.'

A detailed investigation had been undertaken into the circumstances surrounding Corporal Budd's death. An examination of his bullet-ridden body revealed that the ammunition used was of the calibre employed by British forces.

Pathologists who conducted a forensic examination of his wounds also concluded that they were inflicted by British bullets. The only explanation other than friendly fire was that

Taliban forces stole British weapons or bought NATO equipment on the black market.

'Although we've been told about the other possibilities, these seem highly unlikely,' said a spokesman for 3 Para. 'The fact the family have been told there is a possibility of a blue-on-blue means that this is the conclusion to which the investigation is leading.'

Lieutenant Colonel Tootal said, 'Given the dynamics of close-quarter combat that we experienced in Afghanistan, there is always the possibility of casualties caused by friendly fire. However, this does not in any way detract from the utmost valour of Corporal Budd's actions, which led to the winning of his VC.'

General Sir Antony Walker, former deputy chief of the Defence Staff, said, 'Blue-on-blue or friendly-fire engagements are more common on operations than people think. They are always tragic mistakes but are almost always made in good faith. If there is negligence involved that must be investigated. But if it was a heat-of-battle incident I do not see the need for a witch hunt. Whatever happened, nothing can detract from the valour and gallantry of Corporal Budd, who thoroughly deserved his posthumous VC.'

Bryan Budd was cremated at Woodlands Crematorium, Scunthorpe, Lincolnshire.

CHAPTER THIRTEEN

MAORI WARRIOR

CORPORAL BILL APIATA
2004

The exact date of the action that led to Corporal Bill 'Willy' Apiata's award of the VC has not been released to the public. Nor, indeed, have the names of the two other men with him in the action, who also received medals for gallantry, been publicly announced. All three are members of the New Zealand SAS and their actions must, therefore, remain secret. However, on 2 July 2007, the Governor-General of New Zealand, Anand Satyanand, formally announced that the Queen has approved their gallantry awards.

Thirty-five-year-old Corporal Apiata was the first recipient of the Victoria Cross of New Zealand, which was instituted in 1999 to replace the British Victoria Cross for future awards to New Zealand military personnel. Like its forerunner, it is the premier

New Zealand award for courage, awarded for 'most conspicuous gallantry, or some daring or pre-eminent act of valour, self sacrifice or extreme devotion to duty in the presence of the enemy or of belligerents'. There are three other awards for gallantry in the New Zealand honours system: the New Zealand Gallantry Star, the New Zealand Gallantry Decoration, and the New Zealand Gallantry Medal. It was these last two awards that were given to the two other members of Corporal Apia's SAS unit.

The medal and ribbon for the Victoria Cross for New Zealand are identical to the British Victoria Cross instituted in 1856. A total of 21 of the British Victoria Crosses and one Bar have been awarded to New Zealanders. Like the former recipients, Corporal Apiata will be entitled to use the letters VC after his name. He is the first New Zealander since World War Two to win the Commonwealth's highest award. The last New Zealander awarded a Victoria Cross was Squadron Leader Leonard Henry Trent who received it in 1946 for gallantry over Amsterdam in 1943 when he guided a formation of Ventura bombers to their target while under continuous attack from German fighters. Corporal Apiata is at the time of writing the only living New Zealander to hold the award.

The Royal Warrant which governs the New Zealand Gallantry Awards makes it clear that the Queen will approve a gallantry award only on the recommendation of the prime minister. The original commendation had come from former Chief of the New Zealand Defence Force, Air Marshal Bruce Fergusson but, before Prime Minister Helen Clark was prepared to make the recommendation, a huge amount of work had to be done to document what had happened and to research the precedents for the award of the Victoria Cross. In the case of the award of the Victoria Cross, it is also a requirement to consult the Palace, which reflects the historical and international standing of the Victoria Cross.

'Having considered all the information placed before me, having received the strong recommendation from the New Zealand Defence Forces, and having consulted with the Palace, I have decided to recommend to the Queen that the Victoria Cross of New Zealand be awarded to Corporal Apiata,' said Prime Minister Clark.

'Corporal Apiata carried a severely wounded comrade over 70 metres across broken, rocky and fire-swept ground, fully exposed to the glare of battle, heavy opposing fire and into the face of return fire from the main New Zealand troops' position,' Clark told reporters. 'This brave action saved his comrade's life.'

Apiata said he was 'overwhelmed' by the honour.

'At the time I was just doing what I've been trained for,' he told reporters, adding he had only been 'looking out for my mates'.

'I see myself as Willy Apiata. I'm just an ordinary person and this is me,' he said.

For their actions in Afghanistan in 2004 Corporal Apiata's unit also won a presidential citation from US President George W. Bush.

Bill Henry Apiata was born on 28 June 1972 in Mangakino in the Waikato on New Zealand's North Island. His birth certificate carries the first name 'Bill' but he is universally known as Willy. His father is a Maori New Zealander and his mother a *Pakeha* (European) New Zealander. His parents separated but, while he is close to his mother, he has not had contact with his father for several years. Bill has three sisters and is the third youngest in the family.

He spent his early years in Northland in Wellington before moving to Te Kaha in the eastern Bay of Plenty. There, he attended the Whanau-a-Apanui Area School, which he left aged 15. At 16, his mother sent Bill to live with close relatives in Auckland.

In October 1989, Bill enlisted in the New Zealand Army as a part-time Territorial Force soldier in the Hauraki Regiment of the Royal New Zealand Infantry Regiment based in Tauranga. He had been encouraged to join by friends already in the TF.

He first became aware of the New Zealand Special Air Service (NZSAS) when, as a TF soldier, he acted as a member of the enemy party for a NZSAS training exercise. In 1996, while still in the TF, he tried to join the NZSAS selection but failed the selection.

From July 2000 to April 2001 he served in troubled East Timor as a member of New Zealand's 3rd Battalion Group as part of the United Nations operations there. When he returned to New Zealand, he became a full time soldier, transferring to the regular force of the New Zealand Army. Then, in November 2001, he tried again to join the NZSAS. This time he passed the selection and was inducted into the NZSAS training cycle in early 2002. At the end of his training, he had proved himself an outstanding soldier and became a full member of the NZSAS.

For security reasons, New Zealand authorities have drawn a

veil over his subsequent activities. However, due to the award of the Victoria Cross, it is known that he was in Afghanistan with his unit in 2004, following an announcement by the New Zealand government that 50 SAS troops would be sent to Afghanistan at the beginning of April for 'long-range reconnaissance and direct-action missions'. The deployment was to be for a period of six months. The New Zealand SAS were to join 11,000 US troops in a co-ordinated hunt with 70,000 Pakistani soldiers along the Afghan-Pakistan border for top al-Qaeda and Taliban leaders. Prime Minister Clark reversed the normal policy of keeping SAS troop deployments secret. While not going into detail, she said that they would be working with soldiers from other countries and contributing their skills in reconnaissance, surveillance and tracking.

Details of the actions that led to Corporal Apiata winning the Victoria Cross come from the citation:

Lance Corporal (now Corporal) Apiata was, in 2004, part of a New Zealand Special Air Service (NZSAS) Troop on patrol in Afghanistan, which laid up in defensive formation for the night. At approximately 0315 hours, the Troop was attacked by a group of about 20 enemy fighters, who had approached by stealth using the cover of undulating ground in pitch darkness.

Rocket-propelled grenades struck two of the Troop's vehicles, destroying one and immobilising the other. The opening strike was followed by dense and persistent-machine gun and automatic rifle fire from close range. The attack then continued using further rocket-propelled grenades and machine gun and rifle fire.

The initial attack was directed at the vehicle where Lance Corporal Apiata was stationed. He was blown off the bonnet by the impact of rocket-propelled grenades striking the vehicle. He was dazed, but was not physically injured. The two other vehicle crew members had been wounded by shrapnel; one of them, Corporal D, was in a serious condition.

Illuminated by the burning vehicle, and under sustained and accurate enemy fire directed at and around their position, the three soldiers immediately took what little cover was available. Corporal D was discovered to have sustained life-threatening wounds. The other two soldiers immediately began applying basic first aid.

Lance Corporal Apiata assumed command of the situation, as he could see that his superior's condition was deteriorating rapidly. By this time, however, Lance Corporal Apiata's exposed position, some 70 metres in front of the rest of the Troop, was coming under increasingly intense enemy fire. Corporal D was now suffering serious arterial bleeding and was lapsing in and out of consciousness.

Lance Corporal Apiata concluded that his comrade urgently required medical attention, or he would likely die. Pinned down by the enemy, in the direct line of fire between friend and foe, he also judged that there was almost no chance of such help reaching their position. As the enemy pressed its attack towards Lance Corporal Apiata's position, and without thought of abandoning his colleague to save himself, he took a decision in the highest order of personal courage under fire.

Knowing the risks involved in moving to open ground, Lance Corporal Apiata decided to carry Corporal D single-handedly to the relative safety of the main Troop position, which afforded better cover and where medical treatment could be given. He ordered his other colleague, Trooper E, to make his own way back to the rear.

In total disregard of his own safety, Lance Corporal Apiata stood up and lifted his comrade bodily. He then carried him across the 70 metres of broken, rocky and fire swept ground, fully exposed in the glare of battle to heavy enemy fire and into the face of returning fire from the main Troop position. That neither he nor his colleague were hit is scarcely possible. Having delivered his wounded companion to relative shelter with the remainder of the patrol, Lance Corporal Apiata re-armed himself and rejoined the fight in counter-attack. By his actions, he removed the tactical complications of Corporal D's predicament from considerations of rescue.

The Troop could now concentrate entirely on prevailing in the battle itself. After an engagement lasting approximately 20 minutes, the assault was broken up and the numerically superior attackers were routed with significant casualties, with the Troop in pursuit. Lance Corporal Apiata had thereby contributed materially to the operational success of the engagement. A subsequent medical assessment confirmed that Corporal D would probably have died of blood loss and shock, had it not been for Lance Corporal Apiata's selflessly courageous act in carrying him back to the main Troop lines, to receive the immediate treatment that he needed.

New Zealand Defence Force chief, Lieutenant General Jerry Mateparae, said of Corporal Apiata: 'In one respect he is an outstanding soldier, but in another respect he is also just an ordinary New Zealander and a humble man. When he was advised he had won the Victoria Cross he said to his commanding officer: 'I was only doing my job boss'.'

The medal was presented by Governor-General Satyanand at a special ceremony at Government House in Wellington in July 2004, along with gallantry awards to the three other members of the SAS unit on the same mission.

Defence Minister Phil Goff said it was the extraordinary nature of the award that led authorities to release the name of a serving SAS soldier.

'The granting of a Victoria Cross is such an extraordinary event that it would be impossible to maintain the confidentiality of the identity of Corporal Apiata,' he said. 'We came to the judgment that it was better we announce his name and the circumstances of his winning the award, rather than risk the highly probable outcome that it would be leaked somewhere down the track.'

Through his father Corporal Apiata affiliates to the Nga Puhi *iwi* – or tribe – but as he has spent so much time in the Eastern Bay of Plenty, he feels very strong affiliation to Whanau-a-Apanui, the *iwi* of his partner and mother of his child. His home *marae* is Tukaki Marae in Te Kaha. Co-leaders of the New Zealand Maori Party, Dr Pita Sharples and Tariana Turia, expressed their enormous pride in Corporal Apiata's award.

'All New Zealanders can be proud of the leadership demonstrated by Corporal Apiata, in carrying an injured soldier to safety, whilst under fierce and prolonged attack,' said Dr Sharples.

Mrs Turia added: 'Corporal Apiata is known as inspiring his peers, and serving above the call of duty throughout his military career. With this award today, we now know that his courage has been recognised by the Queen as worthy of the supreme award for valour. He demonstrated that extraordinary quality of being prepared to sacrifice his own safety, in order to save the life of his comrade.

'What's more, is that with this award, Corporal Apiata becomes one of only thirteen living recipients of the Victoria Cross – and the only New Zealander in that group. We also remember at this time the only other Maori soldier to receive the Victoria Cross, Second Lieutenant Te Moana-nui-a-Kiwa Ngarimu of Whanau a Apanui and Ngati Porou.'

Lieutenant Ngarimu won his VC in Tunis in March 1943. Until the end of World War Two, men from all quarters of the Empire were expected to risk their lives for the Motherland. Since then, it has seemed an odd thing to do. But the 'War on Terror' has brought Commonwealth troops back onto the battlefield. Sad to say, in the unstable post-9/11 world, our soldiers are not being starved of the opportunity to demonstrate supreme valour under enemy fire.

Corporal Apiata, it seems certain, will not be the last man to win a Victoria Cross.

CHAPTER FOURTEEN

'IT'S INSTINCT, IT'S NATURAL'

TROOPER MARK DONALDSON

2 September 2008, Australian Special Air Services Regiment

The first Australian winner of the Victoria Cross since the Vietnam War, Mark Donaldson, proved on the battlefields of Afghanistan that he was a natural born solider. However, family and friends were surprised when he enlisted in the Australian Army at the age of twenty-three.

Born in Waratah, a suburb of Newcastle, New South Wales, on 2 April 1979, Donaldson entered training at the Army Recruit Training Centre, in Kapooka, New South Wales. The son of a Vietnam veteran, he won prizes as the best shot and the best at physical training in his platoon. Joining the Royal Australian Infantry Corps, he was posted to the infantry school at Singleton, New South Wales. At the end of his training there, he was again given awards as the best shot and best at physical training, as well as the award for being the most outstanding soldier in his platoon.

In November 2002, he was posted to 1st battalion, Royal Australian Regiment, Townsville in Queensland. But Donaldson was determined to excel and decided to pursue his ambition to join the elite Special Air Service Regiment.

In February 2004, he successfully completed the gruelling Special Air Service Regiment selection course and was posted to the regiment that May. With I Troop, 3 Special Air Service Squadron, he was deployed on operations in East Timor, Iraq and Afghanistan.

Then, on 12 August 2008, Corporal Donaldson was conducting night-time operations in Oruzgan Province, central Afghanistan, when the armoured vehicle he was in hit an improvised explosion devices and he suffered minor injuries.

'I was on a Bushmaster at the time, and that thing saved my life,' he said.

Despite his injuries, he continued his deployment. Three weeks later, he was with a convoy of Australian, American and Afghan vehicles that were returning from an operation where they had killed thirteen Taliban fighters when they ran into an ambush. A large Taliban force, armed with machine guns and rocket propelled grenades, were dug in and the Coalition armoured patrol came under heavy fire. They suffered heavy casualties and found themselves on the back foot.

However, the SAS men managed to regain the initiative. Moving rapidly between positions of cover, Trooper Donaldson engaged the enemy with 66mm and 84mm anti-armour weapons as well as fire from his M4 rifle. He also deliberately exposed himself to draw off enemy fire from wounded soldiers, allowing them to be moved to relative safety.

Still with the upper hand, the enemy employed the tactic of the rolling ambush. The patrol was forced to conduct a number vehicle manoeuvres under intense enemy fire over a distance of around two-and-a-half miles (four kilometres) to escape the engagement. This was all the more difficult and dangerous as the vehicles were filled with the wounded, so those who were still able-bodied, including Trooper Donaldson, had to run alongside the vehicles, fully exposed to enemy fire.

As the convoy was being extracted, it was realised that the coalition force interpreter, who was severely wounded had inadvertently been left behind. With complete disregard for his own safety, Trooper Donaldson crossed some eight metres (87 yards) of exposed ground on foot to rescue the wounded interpreter. This drew intensive machine-gun fire from the Taliban in their entrenched positions. Reaching the wounded man, Trooper Donaldson picked him up and carried him back to the vehicles, then provided immediate first aid before returning to the fight.

'I just saw him there, I went over and got him, that was it,' Donaldson explained.

His action undoubtedly saved the man's life.

The engagement lasted over two hours. During that time, Trooper Donaldson administered medical care to other wounded soldiers, while continuing to engage the enemy.

Eventually the convoy made a clean break and got clear of the enemy fire. The ambush had resulted in nine Australian soldiers being wounded, the most casualties suffered in a single action since the Vietnam War.

As Donaldson was with the SAS regiment, he was referred at first as 'Trooper F' when Major General Tim McOwan briefed the press on the 524 days of operations the Australian special forces had undertaken in Oruzgan province, where they had sustained some fifty injuries – some life-threatening. Despite the convention of keeping the identities of SASR soldiers secret, Major General Owen singled Donaldson out for special praise.

'One soldier, whom I shall refer to as Trooper F, moved between positions of cover to engage the enemy, using anti-armour weapons as well as his personal weapon,' he said. 'The soldier deliberately exposed himself to enemy fire on several occasions in order to draw fire away from those soldiers who were already wounded in the initial heavy fire. Without prompting and without regard to his own safety, Trooper F went back to recover the wounded Afghan. He ran across about 80 metres of fire-swept and exposed ground, drawing intense and accurate machinegun fire from the entrenched enemy positions.'

For his acts of exceptional gallantry in the face of accurate and sustained enemy fire, it was decided that Trooper Donaldson would be awarded the Victoria Cross. Consequently, his anonymity had to be lifted when he was presented with the medal by the Governor General of Australia, Quentin Bryce, at an investiture ceremony at Government House, Canberra, on 16 January 2009. The citation read:

For most conspicuous acts of gallantry in action in a circumstance of great peril in Afghanistan, as part of the Special Operations Task Group during Operations Slipper, Oruzgan Province, Afghanistan.

The last Australian VC winner, Kevin Payne, said: 'Your chances of coming out alive are pretty negative, and he never got hit, that's amazing.'

Donaldson was typically self-effacing.

'I'm a soldier, I'm trained to fight ... it's instinct and it's natural,' he said.

The Governor General described Trooper Donaldson as an 'inspiration' and went on to praise Trooper Donaldson further, saying, 'we are here to dedicate your contribution, your unconditional surrender to duty and humanity, your abandonment of your own necessity so that others may be secured.'

Donaldson described the ceremony as 'quite emotional and overwhelming ... it's very humbling'.

After the ceremony, Trooper Donaldson was saluted by Chief of the Defence Force Air Chief Marshal Angus Houston in keeping with military protocol.

'As the highest-ranking member of the defence force, there has been no current serving member that I salute, until now,' he said. 'Tradition holds that even the most senior officer will salute a Victoria Cross recipient as a mark of the utmost respect for their act of valour.'

In fact, Donaldson had received the first Victoria Cross for

Australia. This superseded the British Victoria Cross and is now the highest award in the Australian honours system. It was created by letters patent signed by Queen Elizabeth II, the head of state of Australia, on 15 January 1991, and is the 'decoration for according recognition to persons who, in the presence of the enemy, perform acts of the most conspicuous gallantry, or daring or pre-eminent acts of valour or self-sacrifice or display extreme devotion to duty'.

It takes precedence in Australia over all orders, decorations and medals, and may be awarded to members of the Australian Defence Force and to other persons by the Governor General, with the approval of the sovereign, at the behest of the Australian Minister for Defence. The recipient is allowed to put the letters VC after their name. The medal itself is identical to the British award.

More honours soon followed. On 10 November 2009, Trooper Donaldson was granted an audience with the Queen in Windsor Castle.

'I feel very proud to be given the opportunity to meet Her Majesty the Queen,' he said. 'It's something not many people get do, so I feel very privileged.'

In London he met other members of the Victoria Cross and George Cross Association and, with Lance Corporal Johnson Beharry VC, he laid a wreath in Westminster Abbey on Remembrance Day at a service honouring the last three veterans of World War I – Bill Stone, Henry Allingham and Harry Patch – who had recently died.

By coincidence, Sabi, an Australian Special Forces Explosive

Detection Dog, who went missing during the ambush, was returned that day. Listed as missing in action for over a year, the black Labrador had been spotted by an American soldier with a local man. Suspicious, the GI used voice commands to ascertain that the dog had military training. He knew that the Australians were missing a dog, so she was then flown back to her Australian base in Tarin Kowt, where her handler confirmed the dog was Sabi.

'She's the last piece of the puzzle,' said Trooper Donaldson. 'Having Sabi back gives some closure for the handler and the rest of us that served with her in 2008. It's a fantastic morale booster for the guys.'

Then the following January he was named Young Australian of the Year. 'His bravery in the face of great danger saved lives and won him the highest respect,' the National Australia Day Council said.

After passing a junior leader's course, Donaldson was promoted to corporal. In the mean time, he had returned to Afghanistan, undertaking his normal duties as a SAS trooper with the Special Operations Task Group. But then he was diverted by the other responsibilities that come with his award.

'Obviously I can't attend all events to which I am invited, but it has always been my intention to try and fulfil my obligations, which I take very seriously, to the best of my ability,' he said.

Corporal Donaldson had to request permission off Air Chief Marshal Houston and Chief of the Army Lieutenant General Ken Gillespie to remain a member of the SASR and participate in operational postings. He does not see himself as a hero.

'I still see myself as a soldier first and foremost,' he said.

But Australia's Prime Minister Ken Rudd insisted that he was 'the stuff of Australian legend'.

'Generations of school children will now know of the story of Trooper Mark Donaldson,' said Prime Minister Rudd. 'It is a story of a hero, one which will be told in classrooms, workplaces and watering holes for many years to come.'

Donaldson's wife, Emma, admitted to being afraid for his safety, but said she always believed her man would come home because he was so well-trained.

'He was married to the army before he married me, and I support him all the way,' she said.

Corporal Donaldson had a long association with the army before he joined up. His father, Greg Donaldson, had been with 176 Air Despatch in Vietnam before Mark was born. At the age of forty-seven he died suddenly of a heart attack while in a dentist' chair. This sent his sixteen-year-old son, who was described as 'mischievous', 'carefree' and 'creative', into a period of dark introspection.

Mark and his older brother Brent suffered another tragedy three years later when their mother Bernadette went missing. She is now presumed murdered. Mark, who was then in art college in Sydney, left after only six months. He then went through a series of manual jobs that took him from working on power lines in the Snowy Mountains to making artificial snow in Canada.

His decision to join the army came as a shock to those who knew him growing up, when he was known for his sense of fun and wild streak.

'When I was sent a letter telling me he'd joined the army I just fell off the chair,' said Bob Denner, a member of Legacy, an organisation that takes care of the dependents of former service personal who helped look after Mark and Brent when their father had died. Denner became Bernadette Donaldson's legatee, and the boys became junior legatee wards at the Coffs Harbour Legacy Club.

'He'd sort of slipped away before the Higher School Certificate,' said Denner. 'And I just thought Mark was not the sort of person to join the army at all. He was fiercely independent, a typical country boy. And there was a real softness about Mark, too. I remember he "inherited" a Kelpie puppy, shortly after the loss of Bernadette, which he loved. But he wasn't someone, from my recollection of his relationship with his dad, who responded to discipline and conformity.'

When one old school friend saw 'a clean-cut, super-fit looking' Donaldson on the television receiving his Victoria Cross he could barely believe how different he was from the student he had known at Dorrigo High School who was 'an anti-authority, anti-military sort of guy with wild hair', and 'painted black pictures of skulls.'

Because of Donaldson's appearance back then, the other kids had wanted to pick on him. However, his skill at martial arts meant they did so at their peril.

His brother Brent believes that the loss of the parents may

have played a part in Mark's grace under fire. 'I think for us it gave us a more steely resolve and a stronger-than-average coping mechanism,' he said.

Nevertheless, Brent was surprised when his brother joined the army. 'He was definitely good at art, and that's a tack we were thinking he might take,' said Brent. 'But he still always had loved running, and being outside. And being in a country town you do a bit of everything. You don't specialise like you do in cities, just finding friends who like one thing, because if you did you'd have no friends.'

Looking back, family friend Jo Beaumont saw the logic of Mark Donaldson's transformation from teenage rebel to highly decorated soldier. 'He got a bit rebellious there at one stage,' said Beaumont, 'but nothing out of the ordinary, and it probably had a lot to do with losing his mum, as it would. But at fifteen I didn't ever think he'd take an army career. But there's probably another family for him there in the army, in the SAS, the discipline of his dad.'

Two months after the action where Trooper Donaldson won the VC, the police reopened the case of his missing mother, digging in bushland without success. Back in 1998 traces of her blood had been found in the car of Christopher Watt, a man who had befriended Donaldson's widowed mother. Watt committed suicide by drug overdose in Brisbane a few days after she went missing.

Despite the new investigation Donaldson said nothing to his comrades in arms.

'I know Mark is very, very private, which is something I want to respect,' said Beaumont. 'At the ceremony I was talking to another SAS soldier who was at our table, and he asked me, "Where are Mark's parents?" Mark hadn't even told him.'

CHAPTER FIFTEEN

THE SNIPER'S TALE

BEN ROBERTS-SMITH

11 June 2010, Australian Special Air Services Regiment

The son of Major General Leonard Roberts-Smith, former Judge Advocate General for the Australian Defence Force, Benjamin Roberts-Smith joined the 3rd Battalion of the Royal Australian Regiment as a lowly rifleman in 1996. However, his skill with the rifle resulted in him becoming the most highly decorated serving member of the Australian Defence Force, or indeed any Commonwealth force. When he received his Victoria Cross on 23 January 2011, he already had the Medal for Gallantry, the third highest award in the Australian honours system, which is given to 'military personnel for acts of gallantry in action in hazardous circumstances'. Only forty-seven have been awarded.

In 3RAR Rifleman Roberts-Smith became the section

commander of a Direct Fire Support Weapons platoon. In that role, Lance Corporal Roberts–Smith was deployed twice as part of the Rifle Company Butterworth Malaysia, and conducted two operational tours of East Timor in 1999.

In 2003, he completed the Special Air Service Regiment selection course. He was then cycled as reinforcement until he was given a permanent posting with 3 Squadron. There he served as a member of the Tactical Assault Group West and the Contingency Squadron. He also served as a member of a number of training and assistance teams throughout South East Asia. He went on operations to Fiji in 2004, and served with a number of personnel security detachments in Iraq in 2005 and early 2006.

Later in the year, he was sent to Afghanistan as part of the Special Operations Task Group, where he was a sniper with Task Force 637, as part of Operation Slipper in Oruzgan Province. On 31 May 2006, he was sent with a patrol to establish an observation post near the Chora Pass overlooking an Anti-Coalition Militia sanctuary in extremely rugged terrain. Infiltration up the side of a mountain took ten hours on foot. Their job was to co-ordinate air support for other Special Forces units in the valley below.

After three days, the observation post had become the focus of attention for the Anti-Coalition Militia. They made repeated attempts to locate and surround the position. When the enemy tried to outflank the observation post, Roberts–Smith and his partner moved out of their relatively secure position to locate and neutralise the militia, and regain the initiative.

With the enemy halted on one flank, two more militiamen tried to attack the observation post from the other flank. Again Roberts-Smith moved out to neutralise them. He then realised that the forward edge of the observation post was not secure and made the decision to split his team, taking up an exposed position forward of the patrol so he could use his sniper rifle more effectively. Isolated in this precarious position, he saw a group of sixteen militiamen advancing across open ground towards the observation post. With his sniper rifle, he halted their advance, even though he was receiving accurate small-arms fire from another group of militiamen to his flank. For twenty minutes, Roberts-Smith held this position without support, securing his patrol's position and robbing the enemy of the initiative. He was eventually reinforced by his sniper partner and together they continued to hold off the militia advance for a further twenty minutes until air support arrived.

The citation on his Medal for Gallantry went on to say:

Lance-Corporal Roberts-Smith's actions on the 2 June 2006, whilst under heavy Anti Coalition Militia fire and in a precarious position, threatened by a numerically superior force, are testament to his courage, tenacity and sense of duty to his patrol. His display of gallantry in disregarding his own personal safety in maintaining an exposed sniper position under sustained fire with a risk of being surrounded by the Anti Coalition Militia was outstanding. His actions, in order to safeguard his patrol, were of the highest order and in keeping with the finest traditions of Special Operations Command Australia, the Australian Army and the Australian Defence Force.

Roberts-Smith stayed on in Afghanistan until September 2006, returning to the SOTG again the following year. He was posted to the Selection Wing of the Operational Support Squadron where he helped train SASR reinforcements. In 2009, he was posted to 2 Squadron and deployed as a patrol second-in-command in Afghanistan. He then completed the SASR Patrol Commanders Course and was again deployed with the SOTG in Afghanistan in 2010.

On 11 June, a troop of the Special Operations Task Group conducted a helicopter assault into the village of Tizak in the Shah Wali Kot region of northern Kandahar province, with the aim of capturing or killing a senior Taliban commander. But as soon as their feet hit the ground, they came under machine-gun and RPG fire from the high ground around them. Two soldiers were wounded, and the rest of the troop were pinned down by fire from three machine-guns in a fortified position on the high ground to the south of the village. Under the cover of close air support, suppressive small-arms and machine-gun fire, Roberts-Smith and his patrol manoeuvred to within seventy meters (77 yards) of the enemy to neutralise their machine gun positions and regain the initiative.

During the assault, the patrol drew very heavy and sustained fire. Nevertheless Roberts-Smith and his patrol members fought their way forward until, at a range of just forty meters (44 yards), the weight of fire prevented further advance. Roberts-Smith then noticed an insurgent about to throw a grenade at his patrol and kill him at point-blank range. But two members of his patrol were pinned down by the three enemy machine-gun positions, as bullets ripped up the ground around them.

'One of them was copping a lot,' said Roberts-Smith. 'He couldn't even fight back, couldn't move. At that point I decided I'd had enough. I wasn't going to wait until someone got hit.'

By breaking cover, and drawing fire away from his patrol, he allowed his comrades to return fire. Crawling along a low stone wall that was shielding the enemy, he killed one insurgent at close range and then drew fire from the machine-guns, allowing a colleague to silence one of the machine-guns with a grenade. Seizing the initiative, Roberts-Smith stormed the enemy position with a total disregard for his own safety and killed the two remaining machine-gunners.

This courageous act enabled his patrol to break into the enemy position and to lift the weight of fire from the remainder of the troop who had been pinned down. Seizing the fortified machine-gun position, Corporal Roberts-Smith again took the initiative and continued to assault the enemy. With another patrol member, he engaged and killed one more of the enemy. His action enabled his troop to go on and clear the Taliban from the village of Tizak.

'He just tore into the enemy,' said one of the Roberts-Smiths's friends. 'He is the epitome of the Spartan soldier. It was only a matter of time before he would demonstrate his true ability.'

His action was later compared to the storming of a Japanese

machine-gun post by previous VC winner Edward Kenna in the jungles of Papua New Guinea during World War II.

Corporal Roberts-Smith was awarded the Victoria Cross from the Governor General of Australia, Quentin Bryce, in investiture at Campbell Barracks in Perth, Western Australia.

The citation said:

Corporal Roberts-Smith's most conspicuous gallantry in a circumstance of extreme peril was instrumental to the seizure of the initiative and the success of the troop against a numerically superior enemy force. His valour was an inspiration to the soldiers with whom he fought alongside and is in keeping with the finest traditions of the Australian Army and the Australian Defence Force.

The Governor General went on to thank Roberts-Smith for his bravery.

'Corporal, to use a very Australian expression,' Ms Bryce said, 'it's a big day, but on the 11 June 2010, you saw a far bigger day than this one, the citation distils what you did that day and bears out your awards distinction.'

Australia's Prime Minister Julia Gillard was also at the ceremony and paid tribute. 'Benjamin Robert-Smith you went to Afghanistan a soldier, you came back a hero,' she said. 'From family and school, from mentors and mates and an awareness of the greater tradition than that of his own a greater tradition that binds all of us, a greater a tradition of which he is now part, a tradition called ANZAC.'

At the ceremony, Air Chief Marshall Angus Houston, Chief of the Australian Defence Force, said: 'Today, we in the military feel great admiration and respect for the extreme valour shown by Corporal Roberts-Smith and we are honoured to call him one of our own. In choosing to serve our nation, the men and women of the Australian Defence Force display courage, initiative and self-sacrifice every day. But in Afghanistan on the 11 June 2010, Corporal Roberts-Smith went far beyond what we would ordinarily expect. In the most dangerous and demanding of situations – when his patrol was outnumbered and his life and the lives of his mates were under extreme threat – Corporal Roberts-Smith cast aside concern for his own safety. He placed his mates' lives above his own.'

Again as a mark of respect Air Chief Marshall Houston saluted the Victoria Cross recipient. 'It is a great source of delight to me that, as of today, there are now two serving members of the Australian Defence Force I have the great honour to salute,' he said. 'Corporal Benjamin Roberts-Smith, VC, MG, we are enormously proud of you.'

Chief of Army, Lieutenant General Ken Gillespie remarked on the tremendous humility shown by Corporal Roberts-Smith. 'All Australian Soldiers should feel tremendously proud of the actions of Corporal Roberts-Smith, and the recognition that the award of the Victoria Cross represents,' Lieutenant General Gillespie said. 'The valour of his actions and those of the other members of his patrol, are exemplars of the very best in Australian soldiering. He is a soldier who embodies the Army's values of courage, initiative, and teamwork and the ethos of the Special Air Service Regiment. He is held in the highest esteem by his peers, subordinates and superiors alike for his personal attributes and his professionalism.'

Corporal Roberts-Smith said he was honoured and humbled by the award.

'I am so very proud to have taken part in the action with my mates. This award also belongs to them and to the Regiment,' he said.

'He must be a live one,' said Keith Payne VC. 'The corporal's life will be changed forever and he should not let it affect his character. He should remember to wear it with pride for others. He will now be public property and a lot will be expected of him.'

Later, Corporal Roberts-Smith explained that his actions to protect his team mates were simply instinctive from his military training.

'I think for everyone there, including myself, what's going through your mind is you just won't let your mates down,' he said. 'It's just like being on a football team, you don't let your mates down, you go as hard as you can until the game's won.'

He said he wears the Victoria Cross for his team.

'I saw a lot of brave men do a lot of brave things that day,' he said. 'The decisions I saw made were heroic.'

Others remarked on Roberts-Smith's modesty. Former SAS soldier Rob Maylor, the author of *SAS Sniper*, who worked alongside both Ben Roberts-Smith and Mark Donaldson in Afghanistan, said: 'The three of us have worked together a hell of a lot. We have all worked in Afghanistan and other places. I speak to RS on the phone regularly but he didn't even tell me about what happened in this incident. But I would say he is one of the best soldiers. He is very focused on his job and he is a very, very good thinker. A very lateral thinker. This sort of thing can have a huge effect on someone but he is such a strong character and so humble that, although this is major, it won't go to his head.'

Like Corporal Mark Donaldson, Corporal Roberts-Smith expressed concern that he would not be allowed back in action because of the impact on morale if a VC winner was killed. But neither was happy with a ceremonial or flag-flying role and wanted to be deployed again.

Since the battle at Tizak, Corporal Roberts-Smith had served two length deployments in Afghanistan. He said he had made it clear to his superiors that he did not want the medal to end his career and they had assured him that would not happen.

'I'm a patrol commander in the SAS. I've got blokes underneath me. We're a team and we're expected to do a job and I'm part of that team,' he told *The Australian*. 'I've spoken to the people I need to. Basically, my career will be managed carefully. I'll go wherever they want to send me. I'm a professional soldier. You ask any soldier in the regiment: once you reach patrol commander that is the pinnacle for an SAS operator. You are now the man. You have your own team. The responsibility is yours.'

Corporal Roberts-Smith was also given an audience with the Queen, visiting Buckingham Palace on 15 November 2011. And, like Trooper Donaldson, more honours followed. One of

these honours was being made the number one ticket holder of
the Fremantle Dockers football club; a club he had supported
since it was founded in 1995.

BIBLIOGRAPHY

Adkin, Mark, *The Last Eleven – The Story of the Post-War VCs*, Leo Cooper, London, 1991.

Arthur, Max, *Symbol of Courage – A Complete History of the Victoria Cross*, Sidgwick & Jackson, London, 2004.

Ashcroft, Michael, *Victoria Cross Heroes*, Headline, London, 2006.

de la Billière, General Sir Peter, *Supreme Courage – Heroic Stories from 150 Years to the Victoria Cross*, Little, Brown, London, 2004.

Carew, Tim, *The Glorious Glosters*, Leo Cooper, London, 1970.

Cunningham-Boothe, Ashley, and Farrar, Peter, *British Forces in the Korean War*, British Korean Veterans Association, Leamington Spa, 1988.

Daniel, David Scott, *Cap of Honour: The 300 Years of the Gloucester Regiment*, Sutton Publishing, Stroud, 2005.

Duckers, Peter, *The Victoria Cross*, Shire Publications, Princes Risborough, 2005.

Farrar-Hockley, General Sir Anthony, *The Edge of the Sword – The Finest Hour of the Glorious Gloucesters*, Frederick Muller, London, 1954.

Farrar-Hockley, General Sir Anthony, *The British Part in the Korean War: Volume 1, A Distant Obligation*, HMSO, London, 1990.

Farrar-Hockley, General Sir Anthony, *The British Part in the Korean War: Volume 2, An Honourable Discharge*, HMSO, London, 1995.

Glanfield, John, *Bravest of the Brave – The Story of the Victoria Cross*, Sutton Publishing, Stroud, 2005.

Harvey, David, *Monuments to Courage – Victoria Cross Headstones and Memorials*, Kevin and Kay Patience, Bahrain, 1999.
McLeod, Alistair Sinclair, *Banzai Attack Korea 1951*, New Horizon, Bognor Regis, 1981.

McNeil, Ian, *The Team – Australian Army Advisors in Vietnam 1962–1972*, Australian War Memorial, Canberra, 1984.

Mileham, P J R, *Fighting Highlanders! The History of the Argyll & Sutherland Highlands*, Arms & Armour, London, 1993.

Rambahadur Limbu, *My Life Story*, The Gurkha Welfare Trust, London 1975.

Shipster, John, *Mist Over the Rice-Fields*, Pen & Sword, Barnsley, 2000.

Whiting, Charles, *Battleground Korea*, Sutton Publishing, Stroud, 1999.

Wilsey, John, *H Jones VC – The Life and Death of an Unusual Hero*, Hutchinson, London, 2002.

Woollcombe, Robert, *All Blue Bonnets: The History of the King's Own Scottish Borderers*, Arms & Armour, London, 1980.